Authors' Note

The material in this book is provided to understand the practice of mindfulness. It is not intended to diagnose, treat, or replace potential or ongoing treatments for physical or psychological difficulties. Individuals experiencing physical or psychological difficulties should consult with the appropriate health care provider about their specific needs and discuss whether this approach is best practice for them. It is advised that individuals also consult with their health care provider(s) for any modifications to the practices that may be necessary because of physical or psychological issues.

Mindfulness Starts Here:

An Eight-Week Guide to Skillful Living

Lynette Monteiro, PhD & Frank Musten, PhD

Produced by:

FriesenPress
Suite 300 – 990 Fort Street
Victoria, BC, Canada V8V 3K2

www.friesenpress.com

Distributed to the trade by The Ingram Book Company

Cover Art - enso93 by Lynette Monteiro

Table of Contents

Lynette Monteiro, Frank Musten

Advance Praise

Mindfulness Starts Here is a groundbreaking contribution to the literature on mindfulness in therapy. It explicitly integrates mindfulness techniques into an ethical lifestyle of respect for our mortality and our limits, and for cultivating generosity, compassion, and mindful consumption. The words of these wonderful teachers embody the practice and, together with the companion CD's, provide a comprehensive program for living fully throughout the ups and downs of our lives. When you're ready, here's the trustworthy place you need to begin.

> Christopher Germer, PhD, Clinical Instructor,
> Harvard Medical School, author of *The
> Mindful Path to Self-Compassion & co-editor of
> Wisdom* and *Compassion in Psychotherapy*

Mindfulness Starts Here incorporates the rigor of science, the beauty of art, the wisdom of reflection and years of lived experience. The wealth of theory and practice presented in this illuminating text will be of benefit to clinicians and clients alike, and has the potential to transform our individual and collective lives. I highly recommend it.

> Shauna L. Shapiro, PhD, Associate Professor,
> Santa Clara University, co-author of *The Art and
> Science of Mindfulness: Integrating Mindfulness
> into Psychology and the Helping Professions*

Drs. Lynette Monteiro and Frank Musten have written a gem. This book will be a trusty companion to anyone taking a mindfulness-based stress reduction course or who chooses to independently explore mindfulness practices for an engaged and meaningful life. *Mindfulness Starts Here* is a practical and inviting guide that can help you to make positive changes in how you live your life, starting now.

> Susan Bauer-Wu, PhD, RN, FAAN, Professor
> of Nursing and Religious Studies, University of
> Virginia, author of *Leaves Falling Gently: Living*
> *Fully With Serious & Life-Limiting Illness through*
> *Mindfulness, Compassion, and Connectedness*

Whether you have been practicing mindfulness for many years or for you *Mindfulness Starts Here* is where your introduction to mindfulness begins - you have found a treasure here that you will probably read again and again. This lovely book from Lynette Monteiro and Frank Musten is a beautiful tapestry of wisdom and love that can guide you through life's hardships and awaken in your life greater joy, loving-kindness and well-being.

> Steve Flowers, MS MFT, author of *The*
> *Mindful Path through Shyness* and co-author
> of *Living with Your Heart Wide Open*

In this well-informed and practical guidebook, Drs Lynette Monteiro and Frank Musten share the content and process of their excellent mindfulness-based program with authentic knowledge, simplicity and genuine compassion. Readers will find it engaging and inspiring, bringing the traditional Buddhist teaching of "Right Mindfulness" down to earth and with simplicity. I recommend this book for everyone interested in beginning a well-informed personal practice of mindfulness training and to create or maintain a healthy life, and to all professionals interested in implementing this program.

> Bruno A. Cayoun, DPsych, Director of MiCBT
> Institute and Research Associate at the School
> of Psychology, University of Tasmania, author of
> *Mindfulness-Integrated CBT: Principles and Practice*

Mindfulness Starts Here is a comprehensive invitation to the theory and practice of mindfulness. Weaving ancient Buddhist teachings with practical advice for skillful living, Lynette and Frank offer a step-by-step guide for practicing mindfulness in our lives.

David Dae An Rynick, Roshi, author of *This Truth Never Fails: A Zen Memoir In Four Seasons*

Mindfulness Starts Here is an outstanding text. The authors move seamlessly from a discussion of ethics to very practical and specific exercises, using a tightly organized and beautifully expanded conceptual framework. The depth and erudition of their writing is impressive and results in a work that is in a different league entirely from the common run of programme manuals. As a clinical psychologist, I feel strongly that *Mindfulness Starts Here* has many insights to offer everyone in the profession.

Anne Schlieper, Ph.D., Author of *The Best Fight*

Mindfulness Starts Here has catapulted my knowledge and understanding of Mindfulness to a whole new level. This guide is a wonderful companion to the content of the MBCT groups which I facilitate; what is left implicit in the learning throughout the MBCT program is made explicit in this Guide to skillful living. Lynette and Frank explain the complex and multi-faceted concept of mindfulness, as well as the sources of suffering in life, in such a clear and easy-to-understand manner. The depth and breadth into which the authors go on the topic of mindfulness seems to me to be unparalleled. I will, most definitely, be recommending this guidebook to many of my clients.

Angie Kingma, Occupational Therapist, MBCT teacher at Mindfulness for Health

Dedication

For Alexandra

Acknowledgments

We thank our many generous teachers, colleagues, and friends who have nourished and encouraged us in our practice. In particular, we are grateful for the presence of our daughter, Alexandra Monteiro Musten, who has been patient with our departures and arrivals, always pointing out with wisdom and clarity ways we can be more skillful in body, speech, and mind.

Our spiritual root teachers, Thich Nhat Hanh and Roshi Joan Halifax have blessed us with their generosity in giving away the teachings with an open hand.

MBSR teachers Melissa Blacker and Florence Meleo Mayer, MBCT teachers Zindel Segal, Susan Woods, and Miv London have offered valued training in mindfulness interventions. Steven Hickman and Allan Goldstein of the Center for Mindfulness at UCSD and Bruno Cayoun, founder of Mindfulness-Integrated Cognitive Therapy, have been wonderful friends and supporters of our work. Life Coach and Zen teacher, David Rynick, and Upaya Chaplaincy Director, Maia Duerr, have given us the energy to complete this book and we are honoured to have Maia's generous teaching on meditation in Appendix B.

We are immensely grateful for all who participated in the program at the Ottawa Mindfulness Clinic (OMC). Over a thousand participants in the last ten years have sustained our aspiration to offer an alternative way to deal with suffering. We have been honoured to train many health care professionals in the foundations of Mindfulness-Based Interventions and have grown from their courage and willingness to leap into the heart of mindfulness practices. We bow to their efforts.

We are blessed with an amazing teaching team at the OMC who have encouraged us to follow our path and hold true to our principles. OMC Registrar, Catherine Shaw, has been a priceless gift of patience and care for us and the OMC participants. Many friends have been coerced into reading the early drafts of this guidebook and offered gentle, wise comments. Two in particular, Dr. Anne Schlieper and Susan Kehoe, have hung in through the years of our dithering over words, figures, and format.

We offer thanks and deep bows to the Buddhist communities who have held us to our practice when we have wanted to throw out the incense, put away the bell, and skulk off into the night. In particular, we honour Sr. Annabel Laity and Chân Hội, our dharma teachers and spiritual friends, who always reminded of our commitment to the path of mindfulness.

May the merit of all our practices bring light and compassion into this world.

Lynette Monteiro, Frank Musten

How to Use This Book

We have designed this book to be a free-standing practice manual or a companion to an 8-week Mindfulness program. The chapters follow a typical eight-class program, expanding on some of the concepts and providing the home practice forms that are used in each class.

Although it can be used as a personal practice manual, it <u>does not substitute as a treatment for any mental health disorders or distresses</u>. Please see a trained mental health professional if you are suffering from psychological distress (anxiety, depression, grief, etc.) that is interfering with your ability to cope on a day-to-day basis.

For the meditation practices, you can use the 3-CD set available from the OMC program or substitute one that fits the class practice. The B-E-S-T meditation is available as part of an OMC CD set. See Appendix C for Resources.

We recommend going through the book in sequence. Each chapter lays the foundational practices for the next chapter. It may seem a tad boring to do it this way; however, if we flip back and forth, there is the tendency to encourage a preferential mindset for only those practices that "feel good." Although there is no magical formula that will bring us to well-being, picking only favourites out of the overall practice undermines the intention of meeting all aspects of our experience with openness and curiosity.

Part of the 8-week program includes an all-day session in which we practice mindfulness as a seamless series of transitions. Many meditation communities offer days like this and we recommend you attend one when you are between Chapters 4 and 5 – or when you are ready. There's a description of how to design one for yourself in Appendix E.

Foreword

In today's world, we have the rare and precious teachings and practices of mindfulness that invite us to slow down, stop, and "take a backward step." Mindfulness is not about doing something strange, exotic, or anti-social. It is about letting ourselves open to the depths and richness of the present moment, this very moment, no other than being right here, right now: a miracle in this time when so many are rushing here and there, at great cost to themselves and to the world that all of us share.

This wonderful book, written by Lynette Monteiro and Frank Musten, is an instruction manual for waking up to the present moment. It introduces the reader to the art and practice of living mindfully, of wise mindfulness, and of an ethical field that undergirds the life well and carefully lived. No matter how blessed our life might be or have been, there are always moments when we are touched by stress and suffering. Illnesses, loss, errors in judgment, just plain reality intrude upon us. It is exactly here where mindfulness can take the pain and suffering of the less ideal experiences of being human, and can turn those experiences into teachings. And yes, these teachings can be rare and treasured opportunities. This is what we call "turning into the skid" and mindfulness makes it possible for us to turn into the skid and land safely in the next moment.

The chapters of this book take us through a series of exercises that open the vast field of mindfulness. We begin with our very human body, a veritable treasure house inviting us into awareness. We move then through the fields of our emotions, then sensations. We open ourselves to our thought streams then, and the reminder that "thoughts make the thinker." All these wonderful practices introduced to us can lead us from ill-being to well-being, if we engage them faithfully and whole-heartedly.

Lynette and Frank give the reader and practitioner so many tools for

---

not only survival but human flourishing. Out of this flourishing comes a deep resilience to the challenges we face in our life. It outlines pathways that can bring out the best in us and in the world. I encourage you to follow the sequence they have crafted from their years of experience as teachers. Do the exercises, the practices. This wonderful manual is a step by step method leading the individual through exercises and wisdom that offer so much to us.

Finally, the skill of our authors, who are therapists as well as deep practitioners, is something really important. We are reading the work of people who have worked in very complex and difficult situations. They know their stuff, and we are the beneficiaries of their extraordinary experience.

Roshi Joan Halifax
Founding Abbot of Upaya Zen Center
Director of the *Being with Dying Program*
Santa Fe, July 30, 2012

Introduction

Joy and woe are woven fine
A clothing for the soul divine
Under every grief and pine
Runs a joy with silken twine
It is right, it should be so
We were made for joy and woe
And when this we rightly know
Through the world we safely go.

William Blake

Living skillfully. Living well.

Mindfulness as a word, a concept, and a practice permeates our awareness these days. We learn to be mindful through meditation and intentional attention so that we can cope with the myriad challenges that arise, often unexpectedly, in life[1]. We deeply wish to be able to live well through the good and bad times and we may often feel we lack the skills to achieve that apparently simple goal. In this book, we will work together to cultivate our capacity to live skillfully with careful attention so that living well is the outcome in each moment.

As a word, mindfulness has been around for centuries. In our own lives

---

1   Researcher, author, and mindfulness teacher Dr. Shauna Shapiro has written extensively on the role of intention, attention and attitude in cultivating mindfulness skills.

it would have shown up in the very simple advice given by our grandparents and parents. "Be careful." "Stop and think." "What were you trying to do?" "Wait a second." All of these statements were little bells calling us back to the present moment when we had gone off on some track. They bring us into a state of remembering what we are doing in each moment. In fact, the translation of the original , Sanskrit term for mindfulness, *sati*, means *to remember*.

As a concept, mindfulness is a little more complex. It folds in ideas of being in the flow of things, experiences of fullness, peace and being one with an activity or a scene. There is fluidity in the concept which lends itself to our ideas of Zen-like states although we may not really know what a Zen-like state is. It is a construct that points to our state of mind as we interact with our internal and external environment. Large volumes have been written about this idea and it would be easy to get lost in the intellectual process of trying to understand it.

Jon Kabat-Zinn, founder of the modern movement of mindfulness as a therapeutic intervention, describes mindfulness as "paying attention in a particular way: on purpose, in the present moment, and non-judgmentally" (*Wherever You Go, There You Are*, p.4).

The practice of mindfulness is perhaps the most important in our understanding of mindfulness. Like the idea of riding a bicycle, we can understand it as a word and a concept but until we actually get on that little seat and find the pedals, we haven't begun to truly experience riding. In this book, we will unpack this part of mindfulness, the behaviours that go into creating a practice that leads us in the direction of well-being. We will constantly come back and remember the process of mindfulness as it is relevant to living skillfully: creating an intention to well-being, paying attention to *what is* in this moment, and approaching *what is* with an attitude of curiosity and openness.

In our multi-layered life, there are experiences in which we hold our breath in awe or surprise, where the body vibrates with joy and excitement, or when the mind rests gently like a butterfly landing on an open flower. In those moments we find ourselves fully attentive: open and available as both butterfly and flower, intertwined. In contrast, when we encounter painful times, we close our attention off from the experience. We develop a reluctance to re-engage in the things that remind us of or cause us to revisit those painful moments. Our attention is diverted and distracted, leaving us with a sense of life that is fractured and fragmented.

Being human, our attention is drawn and attaches to sensations that are pleasant and joyful. As they fade, those momentary experiences become an ache and a yearning which drive us in many directions – not all of which lead to good health. We activate our best intentions to live well by trying to recapture the pleasurable moments and avoid the unpleasant ones. However, along with our best intentions, we also need to be skillful in the means we choose to foster well-being.

Our tendency to prefer the lighter, pleasant moments, to block out or run from the unpleasant ones, and to feel restless (bored) when things are neutral is normal (but not healthy). We cultivate living skillfully by the way our body and mind meet the events that occur in our lives. When we are able to enter that interface with an attitude of even-handed observation of what is present, our quality of attention becomes steady, and living well is the outcome.

Joy and woe are part of our lives and there is little we can do to control their appearance. However, in the practice of mindfulness, we learn to focus our attention on how our experience is unfolding, work with what is truly possible in the experience, and cultivate an attitude that nourishes our well-being independent of the valence (positive, negative or neutral) of the experience.

"Right" Mindfulness: Being Mindful of What Is

The typical explanation of mindfulness is filled with stories of peace, serenity, freedom from suffering, and happiness. At best, these stories hold a promise of better things to come; we imagine a future life without suffering from the pain of physical or emotional injuries. At worst, our stories can lead to another disappointment in our attempts to escape the inevitable; the pain may not recede as we had hoped and we are left managing it one more day.

Sometimes, in Buddhist writings, we see the term "Right" Mindfulness. "Right" Mindfulness in this context has nothing to do with our usual understanding of "doing the right thing." "Right" Mindfulness is the process of seeing clearly into our situation, using the wisdom of our experience, and making choices that move us towards our well-being. To practice Right Mindfulness, we cultivate steadiness in the face of challenges so that our wisdom can guide our intentions effectively.

Each of us, as teachers of mindfulness, has met ourselves in that interface between intention and action. In our lives, we have had the invaluable opportunity to continue this practice of *being with what is* which set its roots long before we were even aware of such concepts. We offer below the way in which we were brought to mindfulness, not because our story is a beacon or even typical but because it is a simple human connection with the moments in our experience.

Lynette :

I was born in Burma and grew up in a Catholic/Buddhist family. However, I learned formal meditation practices only during my undergraduate years and used it mainly to manage debilitating anxiety. Over the years, it helped me get through the stresses of university and graduate school, the breakup of a marriage, entering a new career, and beginning a new relationship. Life moved in high gear with a focus on accomplishments as a measure of my success. Yet, for all the accomplishments, I wasn't managing my life very skillfully. Highly driven and always looking for the next hurdle to jump, I found myself brought low by fatigue and ongoing bouts of depression and anxiety. Psychotherapy replaced meditation practices but nothing seemed to bring light into the darkness.

In 1997, I was diagnosed with Fibromyalgia (FMS). The relentless fatigue, struggle to concentrate, unpredictable physical pain, and dark moments could no longer be excused away as the side effect of meeting life's challenges. This cluster of symptoms had a name, a prognosis, and a key to the front door of my life. And, it had booked an indefinite stay. I dealt with the news in a way typical of most driven people: I rejected the diagnosis and went on with life in high gear.

I knew from my own patients with FMS that there was no cure; disability, partial or permanent, was a real possibility. Self-employed and just starting my independent practice three months before, I didn't qualify for disability insurance because this was a pre-existing condition. My thoughts constantly went into a spiral: No work meant no pay. No pay equalled no successful practice and that I had failed. And in my tangled thought spirals it meant life was meaningless. Terrified, I spun into and out of images of catastrophes each time the Fibromyalgia symptoms flared.

Looking for an answer to end this vicious cycle of fear and fatigue, I rekindled my meditation practice and connected with deeply denied emotions. I had silenced so many levels of emotional pain and built a fortress against my feelings. It was no wonder that even physical pain was suppressed automatically. The idea of paying attention to my pain seemed counterintuitive; why would I want to do the very thing I was running away from? Yet as I learned to approach pain with curiosity and gentleness, I learned that the breath conditions every aspect of my being (physical, emotional, and mental) and developed clarity of mind. I also learned that well-being requires a personal ethic which I discovered in the Five Mindfulness Trainings taught by Thich Nhat Hanh. With these insights and practices as my compass, I am better able to be mindful in my health-directed choices: to live deeply, to share, to engage with sensitivity, to speak kindly, and to nourish well. While I don't always succeed, at least my compass allows me to reset my intention when I drift off the path.

Frank:

When I was young, I found refuge in the woods when conflict or life's pressures felt overwhelming. For much of my adolescent years that refuge was a towering, ancient pine near my parent's home in Walkertown, North Carolina. Its branches shaded a small hillock and I used to nestle into a crevice at the hill's apex and wait without moving until the forest returned to life. I would stay quiet watching the squirrels play along the tree branches and listening to the birds as they began to recover their voices. I even learned to enjoy the delicious chill I felt as I tried to discern if the rustle in the leaves near me was a small animal or perhaps a snake. I never quite understood why my mind was so calm after those visits to the tree.

I began in private practice in 1980 when being a psychologist in full time private practice was relatively rare. In those early years, I worked in both Toronto and Ottawa, writing regular columns for magazines, and doing the things one has to do to build a successful private practice. These were exciting times and it didn't seem to matter that I rarely had time to take my canoe out on a lake or just go for a bicycle ride. Periodically, I would find myself feeling emotionally drained and only then would I drag the canoe out and put it in the water for an afternoon. Although I would promise to take more time for myself as soon as work slowed down, I became totally immersed in the turmoil of work and eventually felt completely burned out.

Change and relief came during a Buddhist retreat I attended in 2003. I was desperate to be away from the turmoil but I was apprehensive about the long periods of silence and inactivity. However, I found the silence liberating and the time passed much too quickly. I committed to a regular meditation practice and made it an integral part of my life.

The effectiveness of mindfulness practice was confirmed for me personally as I faced two major exploratory surgeries in the space of six months. While the surgeon did not find the cancer he was looking for, it was a time of tremendous upheaval. The practice of mindfulness anchored me during the turmoil and since then my practice has been to accept the lingering uncertainty, the aftershock of hearing the doctor say, "You may have cancer."

These medical challenges happened as I was integrating mindfulness as a secular intervention in clinical practice and it marked a turning point in my clinical work. I now knew first hand that mindfulness was effective in changing how we meet intense experiences. That awareness helps me to resonate with my patients and I can engage authentically in my work. And, more important, work is no longer a source of burn out. Rather, it is a source of re-generation.

The Coordinates of Skillful Living

Mindfulness-Based Interventions (MBI) integrate three components which are designed to help us deal with psychological and physical distress. Contemplative practices like meditation cultivate steadiness in the face of challenges. Through Buddhist Psychology, we understand that everything changes, that who we are emerges out of a vast complex set of inner and outer experiences, and that avoiding the reality of our situation creates suffering. Theories from Western Psychology propose that our tendency to avoid our experience of pain adds a layer of suffering to our pain. Caught up in that suffering, we lose a sense not just of who we are but, more crucially, of how to stay in contact with who we are becoming in every moment. We experience life sliding past us quickly and irrevocably. We feel ungrounded and disoriented, adrift and without reference points.

In the following chapters, we'll explain some important foundations that map out a mindfulness practice. Mindfulness practices are applied to so many psychological and physical difficulties. They are as varied as leaves in a forest and each leaf has the ability to nourish and effect transformation. However, all mindfulness approaches share a common teaching: the breath and the fundamental aspects of our being are an intricate, interactive map. As we practice moment-by-moment, we will be learning intimately about the coordinates of our map.

Each chapter sets its intention at the beginning, explores one of the foundational concepts of mindfulness, and describes in detail practices that develop mindfulness skills. There are charts in which you can record your observations of and reflections on the different practices. Chapter 1 introduces us to the ways we get dragged off course and offers practices that bring us back on track. As we become more familiar with this map, we can navigate through it with a steady responsiveness to the three realms (Self, Others, World) and to the age-old injunction of *ahimsa* , doing no harm. Chapter 2 explores ways to meet the tough stuff we encounter in our practice – and in life itself. We begin to learn how to meet these roadblocks of tangled thoughts and frazzled feelings with compassion and patience.

Chapter 3 begins the first of the four foundations of mindfulness taking us into our body where we learn how to understand and appreciate how it speaks to us. Learning how to treat our body well is a skill and the practices here bring us into a healthy relationship with our physical nature. We're introduced to the Five Skillful Habits which will be our framework for practice of mindfulness. In Chapter 4 we learn about the second foundation, the true nature of emotions and how to be present to them without becoming overwhelmed or swept away. Chapter 5 deepens our experience of our body's language of sensations, the third foundation. We develop a vocabulary that clarifies our experiences and allows us to know what level of response is necessary to bring us well-being. Chapter 6 takes us into the realm of our thinking brain where we learn about our assumptions and perspectives, the fourth foundation. Here, we learn how mindfulness practice interrupts the automatic behaviours. We also learn about becoming more skillful and cultivating respect for our vulnerability.

Chapter 7 gives us the skills to be compassionate with ourselves. The practices here will help us get a bit of a break from our harsh, judgmental mind. It also opens us to being compassionate to others so that we can enter the rest of our life (Chapter 8) with an open heart and appreciation for this life we have.

The book is set up so that each chapter and its practices build on the previous one just like each class in an 8-week mindfulness program. It does help to do the practices as they are introduced in each chapter but there's no reason to follow it in lock step. We can take what we need. Savor the ideas and the experience. It's more important that we set up our inner and outer space so that we increase the likelihood of enjoying the process. If it falls by the wayside for a day or two, let's not worry. We'll just go to where it was put down and pick it up there. Making these commitments may help:

Being gentle with ourselves. Our internal dialogue tends to be harsh and demanding. We can take the time to remember one or two gentle and understanding words that we have used or heard and incorporate them into our speech.

Speaking to our own experience and from our own experience. We tend to get carried away in our thinking, speech, and actions. This often arises from a need to validate what we feel so we search for other experiences that support our own. We can just feel what we feel.

Taking good care. Physical and emotional distress changes our tolerance for stress. And yes, even a program designed to reduce stress may create additional stress as we shift our schedules around to practice.

A note about our "participants": No one described in the book is a specific participant. (Probably that can be said of our authors too!) The "participants" are a composite of the way many presented their struggles.

Lynette Monteiro, Frank Musten

CHAPTER 1:
The Transparency of Water

Our intention in this chapter: *Our true nature is pristine, like the purest of water. As we hold onto the stories and distractions that we think define us, we lose sight of who we are. We suffer in that loss of vision. Let's look at what brings us to mindfulness, out of suffering, and back to our true self.*

Illness, Stress, and Distress

When we meet people interested in practicing mindfulness, we ask, "So, what brings you to mindfulness?" The usual response is some form of description of a physical illness, the stress of managing work, family, and personal life, or a psychological struggle. We have been privileged to hear stories of loss, grief, spiraling depression, gut-melting anxiety as well as everyday worries, having too little time, lack of connection, and a need to do more or be more for family, friends and self. The theme of all our stories focuses on meeting external demands all the while feeling insufficient to do so.

We live in a time of great progress and much technological wealth. We have access to everything and anything through television and the internet. With laptop computers, tablets, and the ubiquitous smart phones at our fingertips, we are plugged in, wired up, and open to the world which streams a constant image of things against which to measure ourselves. In the face of the type of cars, houses, dishwashers, lawnmowers, and detergents we are told will give us a sense of fulfillment, it's easy to become confused about what we really want or who we really are. And, it's particularly hard to conceptualize or experience our intrinsic worth without the external yardsticks of progress and success. When the definition of success is based on acquisition or external achievement, physical illness becomes a huge roadblock and emotional distress becomes a confusing maze or a frightening secret. We lose sense of who we are, who we intended to become, and what is important in that journey.

Causes and Conditions of Distress

Muddy Waters

Who we are and what we want for ourselves and those we love is created through our experience and through our thinking process. We live an active mental life that seeks out images and builds castles in our inner environment. Then, through hopefully skillful actions, we try to make those dreams a reality in our external environment. One of us may have dreams of being a good parent and that seed is nurtured in our mind with images of things a "good parent" does or says to his child. Another of us may have an idea for a garden or a type of business and begins to formulate concepts which are likely to become a reality with effort. When these dreams, ideas, and concepts are made real, we feel a sense of accomplishment and our vision of being an effective person is clear. When these aspirations meet with obstacles or are criticized as inadequate, we become clouded in our vision of who we are and what we want.

Our mental life is like a glass filled with water and mud. Sometimes the contents are still and settled. We can live adequately with the fact that parts of our life are clear and other parts are mucky with slime and ooze. In fact, many Buddhist teachers say that slime and ooze are crucial to our personal growth. Lotuses begin their life in the mud, cradled and nourished there until the blooms rise above the water clean and untainted by the messiness under water. It's an

> *How mysterious!*
> *The lotus remains unstained*
> *by its muddy roots,*
> *delivering shimmering*
> *bright jewels from common dew*
>
> *Sojo Henjo*

inspiring image because most of us aspire to rise above all the inner turmoil and "ickiness" to be beautiful. We want to be able to roll with the punches, share in the joys of others, and take in a beautiful sunset.

Sometimes, the contents of the glass are stirred up. When we experience anger, anxiety, depression, frustration, grief, loss, or some challenge to our perception of ourselves or others, mud and water mix to form a system that is murky. In these moments, we lose sight of the clarity of water and all we see is a mess of mud. Whatever we have encountered seems to be the entirety of our being. The poet Rumi asked us to invite in as guests depression, meanness, dark thoughts, shame, and malice as a way of learning from these experiences. However, when we are overcome with such muddiness, it feels like these visitors have taken up every nook and cranny of our mind with no room left for love, compassion, joy or kindness. In fact, we can become quite convinced that the clarity of the water that we saw over the mud was an illusion and the muddy mixture is the absolute reality. We come to believe the worst of whoever has hurt us. The roadblock in our career path takes on monumental proportions. The consequence of a lost contract, an upset client, the end of a relationship or of good health seems like the end of our life. We take our unskillful actions as evidence of our unworthiness.

Autopilot

Losing sight of who we are is an easy skill to develop. In fact, we tend to practice clouding our vision as a daily way of being. In order to get things done, we live much of our lives on autopilot. We walk into a room and forget why we went there. We go to the grocery store for milk, buy a bunch of stuff, and forget to buy the milk. We set out on our daily drive to work and can't remember much of the trip there. We feel frustrated with our aging or preoccupation.

Bring to mind your day. When you woke up, were you aware of that moment of growing awareness of what it feels like to be in bed or were you already caught in the activities of the day to come? As you were showering, were you feeling the water on your body or were you already wondering how to get breakfast ready for yourself, your partner and/or your children? At breakfast, were you already in the car? When driving, were you already at that meeting with the boss or colleague that you were dreading? At any given time in the day, we are likely living a time zone or two away. Yet, if asked, we would probably say that we're very aware of what we're doing and where we're going. We have maps, lists, plans, and beeping reminders on our computers or phones to tell us where we are in time and space. In fact, we get indignant if we're told we're not paying attention.

Many years ago when one of us (Lynette) was in the field of assessing and treating children with Attention Deficit Disorder, we attended a workshop given by Ed Hallowell, who wrote *Driven to Distraction*. He commented that many adults with ADHD don't even realize they meet the criteria for the disorder and that the people who can best diagnose the disorder are the partner or close friends of the person. He asked the audience how many of us believed we had ADHD. Both of us looked around at all the people raising their hands; our hands were firmly tucked into our laps. Then Hallowell asked how many in the audience believed our spouse had ADHD. We both raised our hands!

Just as the eye cannot see itself and the hand cannot grasp itself, it is hard for us to be aware of who we are in each moment. The busy mind carries us away at the speed of thought and we live in a world where that busy-ness is valued as something positive. At the same time, multitasking and rapid information processing is a necessity in our fast-paced world. Even as this is being written, the computer is scanning for viruses, updating the firewall program, backing up the files online, and recording the keystrokes. The writer of this paragraph is composing, remembering where the reference books are, mentally reviewing the handouts so that there is consistency with this text, wondering if her daughter is enjoying her vacation, and deciding what to have for dinner. We could also throw in a feeling of anxiety about this whole process of writing a book on mindfulness.

The problem is not that so much is going on in this moment. That's the nature of mind; it's a busy creature that's been described as being like a monkey that's drunk and been stung by a bee. It swings rather wildly at times and there is no predicting where it will end up. Problems arise when the peripheral issues trip up the primary intention. If the writer begins to worry about the purpose of the book, whether the references are where she thinks they are, what people will think of this work, worrying about her daughter and whether she's a good mother if her daughter has a bad vacation and so on, the creative process is now subservient to worry, rumination, and projection into the future. Suddenly, the fingers trip over computer keys, doubt creeps in, and sentence structure goes to mud!

Trains to Nowhere

Going down peripheral paths mindlessly is like getting on the wrong train[2] in our mind. Imagine being in a train station, standing on a platform. When we're on autopilot, we tend to get on trains we ought to let go by. Imagine being in a train station, standing on a platform. We want to take the train to a town nearby and we have a ticket in our hand. The trains are not clearly marked and sometimes they seem to be going to where we want to go. We may be feeling excited about the journey or we may be feeling some anxiety. A train pulls in and, automatically, we hop on. We're on autopilot. A few stations along the way, we realize we're on the wrong train. The scenery doesn't look familiar. Or maybe it does look familiar but it's not pleasant, some place we've been to and want to avoid revisiting. Having acted without awareness, we find ourselves in a state of mind we never intended to visit and the journey back may take a while.

We're born with a large number of train tickets and if we're not mindful about which train to get on, we can spend much of our time wandering the back roads of our experiences and feeling exhausted from having to find our way back home. The thinking patterns we encounter when we feel anxious or depressed are typical of what we mean by "getting on the train." In one moment, we may be feeling sad or blue; in the next moment we're caught in feelings of helplessness and hopelessness.

Mindfulness practices allow us to attend to the nature and direction of the train that pulls into our station. In terms of emotional experience, mindfulness practices allow us to be aware of the early stirrings of a feeling **and** see clearly our choice of actions.

Susan came to the clinic following an episode of depression. She described a history of dealing with highly stressful jobs and family demands including caring for an ill parent. After her parent died, she became unable to cope with the demands of her job. Her belief that her life had not gone in a direction she had envisioned for herself lead her to feel like a failure.

---

2   We gratefully acknowledge Joseph Goldstein for introducing us to the idea of trains taking us into unexpected mental states.

Susan's physician provided her with a certificate for time off work and although it was useful, it also eroded her self-confidence. In her thinking, she diminished herself and judged herself harshly as someone incapable of managing "even the simplest thing like deciding on a grocery list." She had sought psychotherapeutic treatment and found it helpful because she could now go back to work and get through the day's demands. Yet, she was unhappy and afraid.

As we talked, it was clear what was happening: she was no longer as depressed as she had been but she was afraid to feel either better or worse. The fear of relapse and the fear that she may not really be better kept her frozen emotionally. We explored her thinking patterns and Susan noticed that each time she encountered a good day of feeling pleasant or energized, her thoughts were in the tone of "don't trust this" or "be careful or you'll wear yourself out." If she encountered a difficult moment, her thoughts cascaded quickly into "Oh no! It's happening again! I can't concentrate (focus, keep up, understand). I'm going to become so depressed; I won't be able to work again."

As Susan learned about these trains that took her down negative paths – especially the sneaky ones that tell us not to trust ourselves – she began to notice how many trains she got on through the day and how debilitating some of them were for her. She began to label the trains so that she could stop the train to get off and sometimes even recognize them from a distance and not get on. Susan laughed when she noticed that sometimes when on a train, she tended to "transfer" onto a more self-diminishing one. Eventually as her skills in the mindfulness practices increased, she learned to use the trains as useful explorations to understand her ways of thinking and see clearly the choices that were available to her.

Jobs are lost, finances are depleted, friends and family members do leave us. Illnesses are terminal and pain can be unrelenting. These are events that have painful consequences for our health, functionality, and relationships. When we're deep in such pain, it's hard to believe this is only the surface of the challenge to perceptions. At a deeper level, when we are in painful times, our sense of who we are is challenged. This is the common thread that links all of us. Our definition of who we are, our belief of who we would have been under certain circumstances, and our trust in our capacity to effect change in an individualistic way have been shaken.

Not only is our glass of mud and water stirred up and the vision of our true nature occluded, we are terrified that things will never be the same again. When we engage in a practice of mindfulness, we learn to see clearly that one part of this experience is mud and to remember that the other part is still pure water.

Reality of Pain

Physical and emotional pain carries us away from that solid base of comfort and confidence that we build from our experiences. Pain changes our perceptions of ourselves, of others, and of our environment. Pain can be a twinge- a pinprick, a disappointment - or it can be a crashing wave of immense sensations, physical injury, or profound emotional distress. It can last a split second or it can be relentless. It can seem to fill the horizon or it can be a finely sharpened point in the mind. Even the categories of physical and emotional pain become fused as body and mind cross boundaries in trying to manage the intensity of our experience.

Living skillfully with pain challenges us to re-visit our assumptions about permanence, identity, and how we conceptualize our lives. Each time we experience that surge of sensations, we are reminded that life has changed and we are no longer in charge. It may also remind us that we have not taken the stewardship of our life to heart. Living well is the process of seeing change as it is happening. We see that our sense of who we are is shifting continuously. Our ideas of how things "should be" adapt seamlessly to our real experience rather than to the imagined life we live. When pain threatens to derail us, we meet it with an awareness of and openness to all the possibilities that are available in the moment. In other words, well-being is living a personal ethic of doing no harm to ourselves, by extension to others, and hopefully some day to our world.

Well-Being

The Transparency of Water

Water is fascinating in its qualities. It is unconstrained yet containable. It exerts power yet can be held in our cupped hands. It never actually separates from the mud but is not attached to it. It is transparent yet reflects everything in its environment. It holds all manner of flora and fauna yet does not take on the nature of what it carries. It can be cloud, rain, fog, steam, ice, and liquid. It nourishes and is crucial for life.

And so is our true nature.

> To each thing its own
> true deepest inner nature:
> Water does not think
> of itself as the consort
> of the bright moonlight it hosts.
>
> Sogi

When we see only the muddiness in the glass, we forget that the turmoil, the setbacks, the feelings of loss and rejection are being held in the liquid of our true self. We identify with the turmoil and become fearful that it will define who we are. Our tendency is to try and break through, move past, look beyond the confusing mess in front of us. So often, participants tell us, "This is not me. Before the depression (anxiety, cancer), I was not like this." We become distressed because we believe we have lost the purity of water (the real "me"). We lose our sense of direction and purpose because there is no clarity.

In reality, the clarity is still there. The nature of our true self, like the water that holds the mud, is transparent so that we can see clearly what is ailing us. The water itself, our true nature, doesn't become opaque. It remains clear in order for us to look deeply into what we are actually experiencing. Its transparency allows us to recognize the nature of the mud and to investigate it carefully. Whatever our pain, our true nature is not tainted by it. When we can learn to hold the pain, we feel the same way as the water that contains the mud and not being afraid of what it means about us, we are able to peel away the assumptions and the fears it generates. *What are the real issues of this illness, lost job, or relationship? What is within my control and what is not? What am I really feeling: is it anger, withdrawal or disconnection; or is it hurt, rejection or loss?*

Jason was diagnosed with an autoimmune disease that had a relentless course. He had to leave his career and was on long-term disability. Finances were not a concern because, as a lawyer, he had been wise in his investments and savings. His children were adults and not in need of financial support. Life had been very good and his spouse was supportive throughout the initial struggle to reach a diagnosis. When he first arrived for the individual session, he attributed his anxieties to ending his very successful career. He believed that if he could manage the physical pain, he could return to work at some minimal level to satisfy his need for accomplishment. Initially, it seemed a reasonable analysis of his case and certainly fit with the personality style of a hard-driving professional who had contributed almost 30 years to public and community service. As we proceeded through the course, Jason became very good at reading his body's needs and managing the physical pain. However, working on emotional awareness, he began to touch the deep sadness that his connections with his community were slipping away. He was insightful enough to realize quickly that he was living in the future where the disease had run its full course and he was totally debilitated. His stories had built a scenario of abandonment and isolation, which lead him to live as if it had already happened. His trains were powerful turbo-driven trips to lands of desolation and despair, which drove the anxiety to get better physically. As he looked deeper into his experiences, he realized that returning to work – even minimally – was not going to be possible. It was hard for Jason not to feel that everything he had done in his life had been pointless.

With steady investigation, Jason was able to see that his nature was to be generous and connected with people. The disease had not done anything to affect that core nature. What he had to learn was to be skillful about that generosity and to use the symptoms of the autoimmune disease as a mindful bell that moderated his tendency to give too much. He was surprised that giving can be effective even in a moment by moment way. Each conversation with someone whether at a lunch with colleagues or at the grocery store was an act of giving. These moments served to satisfy his need to connect and they replenished him in return. Because he was mindful of the resources he had in each moment, he didn't deplete himself as often and connections were more about "topping up the tank" than "bringing it up to empty".

Our ultimate aspiration is to realize our true nature is constant and not tainted by the pleasant, neutral, and unpleasant life experiences. To do that, we learn how to look deeply into our experiences so that we can develop clarity and steadiness in the face of turmoil. We start by learning different mindfulness skills such as meditation which help us calm and settle our body and mind. As we become skillful, we see the ways in which we live distracted and disconnected from our body, feelings, and thinking. We begin to reconnect body and mind so that we are in an appreciative partnership again. We remember our true self.

Let's stop a moment here to enter that partnership with ourselves. Let's consider what our expectations are of our practice of mindfulness. The exercise "What do I want" is a way of exploring non-judgmentally what our thoughts and feelings are right now. Find a quiet place and give yourself a few moments to look deeply into your hopes for yourself.

Practice: What do I want?

Settle into a comfortable position in your chair and read these two paragraphs all the way through. Then close your eyes and practice. There are many things that have brought you to this point in your life. There were likely wonderful times and difficult times. In this very moment, as you are reading this, many causes have created the conditions that allow you to hold this book, see these words, and experience these ideas. Your friends and family may have created a space that gave you time to explore what you need. You may be concerned enough for yourself that you have set aside work or other enjoyments to learn more about how to better care for yourself. This day, this time, and these words have all come together with effort from you and all those around you so you can have something you want. Here you are. Breathing in, breathing out.

Now gently ask yourself: **What do I want?** When you close your eyes and ask yourself this question, allow the answers to float into your awareness. Don't judge them or form any preference for them. Don't discard any answer as silly or pointless or superficial. Accept them all and gently set each one on a shelf like a precious gift. Keep asking the question: What do I really want? What do I really, really want? Add as many "really" probes into the question as you need until you get to a point where you feel you've heard all the possibilities. Stop here and begin.

Consider your answers. Was there a theme? Did you hit one answer and then no others? Were the answers all different?

Consider the process. Did you notice the judging mind or the skeptical mind? Were you distracted from the questioning process with thoughts of other things? Did you get caught in debate about the "rightness" of what you want?

Consider your relationship with you. Are these reactions typical when you have a chance to see yourself? Does the clarity of exploring what you want get muddied by the inner dialogue and take you away from your connection with yourself?

The Practice of Well-Being

Living Well

The practice of living well is simple. Choose the actions that sustain physical health and joy. Engage in the activities that are useful and beneficial to ourselves and others. Adjust and adapt when conditions change and those activities are no longer useful or beneficial. When we are on autopilot and catch ourselves hopping on a train, we can remember our intention to practice well-being and return to that station with ease.

The practice of living well is not easy. We tend to be distracted or hyperfocused, demanding or disconnected, clinging or disinterested. We believe that we are entitled to certain things in our life that are also a measure of our acceptability or success. Often the actions that grant us those things have a cost. We feel off kilter, off center, tipping too far over into distress and ill health. We become reactive and forget our skillfulness in living well. Our lives are filled with trains that take us nowhere or to destinations that are unpleasant.

Well-being is not the absence of illness or distress. It is the recognition that we are tipping over, remembering where we felt balanced, and returning to that center point. When we act with awareness of what is useful, beneficial and the cost of our choices, we are practicing a skillful way to return to the center. The stronger the skill in remembering and recovering that center, the more skillful we become at practicing well-being.

That process of noticing, remembering, and recovering embodies the practice of mindfulness. We pay attention, become aware, recall past consequences and skillful actions, and make choices in this moment that are based on our belief that living well is the only act of kindness possible for ourselves and others.

Mindfulness

A typical understanding of mindfulness hovers around concepts like "being in the now" or "being aware of this moment." When we try to clarify what it actually means to be in this now, the definitions shift to an outcome or an expectation. Serenity, peace, calm or still are words that are often heard in explanations of what mindfulness means to each of us. Under the words and phrases, there is a deeply felt desire to be at ease, to be free of the struggle we all endure when we're faced with something that seems beyond our capacity to hold.

Let us explore the definitions of mindfulness, not as something conceptual or scientific but as a process of connecting with our well-being. When we bring to mind a moment in which we felt fully present to what was happening in our life, we see that mindfulness is not just about being attentive, aware, or being in this moment. For example, we can be responding in an angry manner and be fully aware of it. We may be saying nasty things that we know later we will regret (or not). We feel fully connected to that anger and that moment. But this is not practicing mindfulness; it is more likely being carried away by past habits, autopilot, and getting stuck on a train about our vulnerability.

We are truly practicing mindfulness when angry, if we notice exactly what "this" moment is filled with and not looking away. We see, hear, taste, smell, or touch whatever is presenting itself to our senses. We hold our attention on that experience, not letting the mind wander off into stories about whether these sensations are good or bad. We recall the consequences in the past when we spoke from that anger. We recall times when we found a different way to deal with our anger. We see the choices available to us and understand which are most likely to be useful and beneficial in resolving the situation.

In order to do all that, we have to take a step back and learn not to be caught in the fury of the moment. We begin by staying calm and noticing what is actually happening. When we meet a challenge, our usual tendency is to react out of fear, anger, or indecision and to generate multi-layered stories about the danger, deprivation, or uncertainty of the situation. These stories are usually created by leaving out certain sensory information and enhancing others. In every event, for ease of processing, our mind carves off the sensations that are not immediately relevant to our survival. We can explore this in the example below.

If you live in a part of the world where you've had the experience of suddenly finding yourself driving on black ice in the winter, you know the feeling of everything going really slowly and the vision sense filling your awareness as the car skids out of control. Or perhaps, if you live in sunnier climes, you've been in a situation where you had to suddenly avoid a potential accident while driving; the sensations of moving in slow motion and tunnel vision would be the same. At that moment, the information about your predicament that is sent to your brain by some of your senses such as taste, hearing, smell and touch are given a lower priority. Vision and the mind take priority to ensure your survival. If you happen to be a seasoned driver or have trained to deal with winter road conditions or defensive driving strategies, you know that staying calm and not reactively stepping on the brakes is the key to bringing the car into control – even if all the information coming in through your vision sense says the opposite.

So the first step to mindfulness is staying calm. This means not being distracted by our automatic ways of dealing with situations. In the situation of driving on ice, it means not getting carried away with thoughts of disaster or becoming caught in any physical sensation like our speeding heart or holding our breath. In the moment of the skid, we have to remember that our vision sense is over-active and our mental activity is in survival mode. As we calm body and mind, our previously learned skills have a chance to engage.

The second step to mindfulness is noticing all the other sensory inputs. We may notice then that vision and the activity of the mind are not the only senses that are active. Breathing, muscle activity, thinking, and proprioception (sensing the movements of the car) are also active. All these other sensations give information and create the potential for a steady response that brings the car into control. Noticing we're holding our breath, we breathe. Noticing our arms are rigid, we unlock the elbows and relax our grip. Noticing our vision has tunneled, we open up to see what obstacles we may have on the road. We may have learned maneuvers in a driving course or through our own experience that are useful in these circumstances. As we engage in these actions, more sensory information is processed allowing us to make additional decisions for a safe recovery.

Mindfulness practice in a nutshell is easily remembered as CARR: Calm, Aware, Remember, and Recover. It can be summed up as an attentive awareness of the entirety of our experience in the moment. Let's begin by learning how to calm our body and mind.

Calming the Mind: Meditation Practice

Most people associate "meditation" with the feelings generated by the process of doing meditation: floating feelings, deepening awareness, opening up, or expansiveness. The techniques that are commonly associated with the term "meditation" are sitting quietly, trying not to think thoughts, and paying attention to our breathing. The mind however has other ideas about all this. As soon as we sit on that cushion or chair, we begin to notice how busy our mind actually is. Our first reaction is to try to strong-arm the mind into submission which only releases a greater flurry of thoughts. It's the nature of the mind to be active, to flow from one thought to another like a monkey swinging from branch to branch in a forest. If it was as simple as that we would probably feel OK about the state of our mind. However, that monkey-mind often acts like it is drunk and been stung by a bee. Imagine if we were to put that monkey in cage; there would be a whole lot of rattling and fury and, not surprisingly, the same thing happens when we try to control our mind in order to quiet it.

So, before we get to enjoy the fruits of meditation we need a bit of "concentration" training. When the mind is busy, concentration practices act to settle the mental activity by providing the mind with an anchor or a focus. Some meditation schools use mantras, some use chanting, some use body movement, some use visualization. Regardless of the specifics, all concentration practices are based on the awareness of the breath. Let's take a moment now and bring our attention to our breath. Notice the flow through our nostrils, the rise and fall of our chest or abdomen. Let's not worry if our breathing is "right" or "wrong." As long as we remember to breathe in after breathing out, it's a good guess that we're doing fine.

There are two things we will learn about the connection of the breath to our way of being. First, the breath is our primary teacher when learning how to train concentration. Because it is a constant feature of our body's functions, it forms a solid anchor that keeps us from drifting too far away in our thoughts.

Throughout the book, we will be practicing a constant refrain of coming back to the breath. That means to bring our attention to the flow of the breath beginning at the nostrils, feeling the sensation of the air flowing in and out, and following that breath into the lungs and abdomen, feeling the expansion and contraction of the chest and stomach areas. Some teachers use a counting method: count each breath in and out up to ten then count back down to one. Each time thoughts or autopilot takes attention away from the breath simply resume from one again. Notice the inner dialogue, the judgments, the harshness, or the high expectations. Notice and return to the breath.

We tend to put a lot of pressure on ourselves to get it right. The beauty of meditation is that there is no right or wrong way. Actually, there is one "wrong way": spacing out is not meditating. If we've lost connection with the breath and full awareness of what we're doing in this moment, we're not practicing concentration and awareness, we're zoning out. Notice it and come back to the breath. Remember it's not about having no thoughts or not wandering off. It's about coming back as soon as we notice we've gone away. In that sense, it's helpful that we do wander off because we can learn to come back.

The intention of concentration practice is to encourage the mind to come back when it has wandered off. In effect, we're teaching it the behaviour it needs to get off autopilot or get off a train under non-stressful conditions. When that behaviour is strengthened under non-stressful conditions, it becomes readily available under stressful conditions.

Second, the breath is a powerful way to condition the body and mind. When the breath is steady and calm, the body is steady and calm. When the breath is agitated or tight, the body responds similarly. We notice the breath is tight and our mind is agitated. We notice that we are caught in our past or our future. We notice that there is a connection between the turmoil and our perceptions of what catastrophe might befall us. We are beginning to understand and have insight into our experience. As we stay with the flow of the breath or the rising and falling of our abdomen, we may begin to notice changes, shifts, and interconnections of breath and being. When we remember to get off trains, come back from our distractions, and feel the connection between our breath and our immediate experience, we are beginning to meditate.

Concentration practice goes hand in hand with meditative practices. In order to notice the interconnections of breath and body, feelings, thoughts, and assumptions about the world, we need first to be able to shine a steady light on the object of our interest. Practicing coming back to breath nine billion times a day is a good start. Then we are developing good skills to notice where we are in our momentary experience and what to do about it.

Awareness

As we gain skillfulness in remaining calm or steady in the face of different challenges, we become more likely to increase our capacity for awareness of the messages from our body and mind as it interacts with the world. Information is communicated through six sense portals which are touch, sight, sound, smell, taste, and thinking. (Thoughts are the activity of the mind and the way in which we create understanding of our connection with our inner and outer environment.) In our usual state of haste and disconnection (autopilot), we tend to not receive these messages very clearly, if at all. Tightness in our neck becomes pinched nerves, tension becomes a migraine, and upset stomachs become ulcers or acid reflux. Signals from our body are usually experienced as vague or undecipherable sensations that are like hearing a different language.

At the other end of the spectrum of experience, if we are experiencing chronic pain, it may seem like our body is sending messages in a rapid fire rate; it may feel like it's screaming at us all the time. As with a real person screaming, it's hard to figure out what's actually wrong and what's needed to resolve the problem. And in all this mix of signals, our mind leaps in with its own version of what is happening, what might happen, and demands to understand why it's happening.

In cultivating mindfulness we begin by learning how to attend to each sensation without allowing the others to interfere. To experience how our senses come together at differing levels of awareness, let's try the practice on Awareness of Our Senses.

Take a moment to prepare a space and be sure you will not be interrupted. Make a commitment that you will not answer the phone (or better yet, turn off the ringer), email notifications, or any other calls to move away from your intention to be good to yourself in this moment. Follow the directions in the box, one paragraph at a time. This too is a practice of mindfulness: stay where you are, resist the impulse to bounce ahead before you have acquired the information available in this moment, this word, this sentence, this paragraph.

Practice: Awareness of Our Senses

(Please respect your allergies to food in this exercise.)

You can practice this exercise with any piece of fruit, fresh or dried. If you are not allergic to nuts, you may wish to try a walnut, almond or pecan. Choose something that you can easily hold in the palm of your hand.

Read this paragraph before you begin. You will start by holding the fruit or nut in the palm of your hand and close your eyes. Breathe in and out counting from 1 to 10 and then 10 to 1 for each breath. Then open your eyes and just look at the fruit in your hand. Continue looking at it for about 30 seconds or so. Then read the next paragraph.

What did you notice about the fruit or nut through the sense of sight? Write down the words that reflect seeing. They can be the colour of the fruit, the light or shadows, the size, the shape, etc. When you're done, read the next paragraph.

Taking the forefinger of one hand, touch the fruit or nut. Roll it around on the palm of your hand. Get a deep sense of what it feels like. Continue to touch it for about 30 seconds or so. Then read the next paragraph.

What did you notice about the fruit or nut that came through the sense of touch? Write down the words that reflect feeling. They may be related to texture, moisture, contour, etc. When you're done, read the next paragraph.

Pick up the fruit or nut and bring it to your ear. Listen for about 30 seconds or so. Then read the next paragraph.

What did you notice about the fruit or nut through the sense of hearing? Write down all the words that reflect hearing. When you're done, read the next paragraph.

Pick up the fruit or nut and bring it to your nose. Breathe in the scent of the fruit or nut for about 30 seconds. Then read the next paragraph.

What did you notice through the sense of smell? Write down the words that reflect smell. When you're done, read the next paragraph.

Place a piece of the fruit or nut in your mouth but don't chew. Feel it on your tongue and against the palate of your mouth. Then very slowly chew once. Breathe three times and chew again. Continue to chew this way slowly and methodically only swallowing when the fruit or nut is completely soft. Then read the next paragraph.

What did you notice about the fruit or nut through the sense of taste? Write down all the words that reflect the sense of taste. When you're done, read the next paragraph.

What did you notice about the sixth sense, the mind. Write down the thoughts you had that reflect the sense of thinking.

The first thing we might have noticed in the exercise is that it's not easy to keep the other five senses from butting in when we're trying to attend to one sensation. Look at the words that were listed for each sense portal. Some may be clearly based in the sense perception such as red, pungent, bumpy, sweet or squeaky. Others may be ambiguous like rough or sticky. Separating smell from taste, touch from sight is tricky even if we're sitting quietly in our kitchen with only this exercise to do. Imagine what it must be like for us to try to figure out what's triggering a stressful reaction when we're in full flight and often on autopilot.

Second, we may also notice that as we persisted with the exercise, it became easier to set aside the intrusions and simply experience whatever sensation was the chosen focus for the moment. The object is not to only feel one sensation but to stay with the one we've chosen as our object of awareness. As we stay with each sense we become more attuned to its unique language and style of communicating. We begin to discern stress from distress, pain from suffering, and our belief about a problem from the actuality of the problem. This is particularly important as we get into the practices later in this book.

Finally, we may have noticed that we gave the final say to the mind sense more often than we realized. We might even have noticed that the mind sense is the worst culprit for trying to steal center stage when other senses are trying to speak to us. It probably had all kinds of ideas and opinions and we might even have gone along with it for a while. The mind sense is tricky because it is both the observer and participant in our experience. We experience sensation through a sense portal (vision/eyes, hearing/ears) but we can only comprehend and render it useful through the mind's interpretation. Learning to be mindful of the mind sensations (thinking) while using the mind to do so is likely the biggest challenge we all face in this practice – and one that reduces many of us to feeling as if we have been mentally hogtied and turned inside out.

For now, however, having an idea of how messages fly back and forth in our body/mind, let's begin to explore the ways we can establish mindfulness in our daily life.

Re-Membering Our True Nature

Our experience in any moment is contained in the Body, Emotions, (physical) Sensations, and Thinking (B-E-S-T). When we are aware of our experience as it is, it's not hard to know that a stomachache is not cancer even if there are fears or thoughts about cancer. However, we tend to live in an internal world where thoughts reign supreme. It's easy to hop on "Trains of Catastrophe" and lose sight of what is a real concern and what may not be. Mindfulness practice develops our skills in knowing what the source of our experience is and how "B-E-S-T" to respond to it.

Let's go back to the train station and look at it more carefully. The station is made up of four platforms: Body, Emotions, Sensations, and Thoughts (B-E-S-T). When we stand on each platform, we are standing in the source of some aspect of our experience. In order to make healthy choices to sustain good health or recover from illness or injury, we must learn to listen closely to what our internal environment is saying to us. Mindlessness prevents us from hearing the communication and often the results are ongoing injuries or a poor prognosis of recovery. Mindfulness skills clear the static and interference, allowing us to listen carefully so that we can see all the possible choices available to us in the moment.

Body

On the Body platform, we experience an awareness of the physical nature of our body. The external structures such as toes, feet, legs, hips, arms, hands, fingers, hair, teeth, and the internal organs like heart, lungs, digestive system, and so on are all part of this platform. The sensing organs such as skin, eyes, nose, ears, and tongue are part of our physical nature as well as being the interpreters of our environment. Here, we are aware of the physicality of our being as it acts as an interface with the environment.

If we are attuned to the physical nature of our lives, we can respond with appropriate care and consideration for what the body needs. (We'll get to how the body communicates that need later on.) Mindfulness of the body means staying on this platform and not hopping on trains to get away from what is happening here.

Ashley came to the clinic because of chronic back pain. She described her body dispassionately as a machine that had broken down yet she expressed feelings of betrayal as if it were a friend. Her words reflected an ambivalent relationship with her body alternating between disregard and frustration. She had gained a lot of weight over the years and had given up her exercise routine as the weight gain made it harder to jog and work out. The back pain was related to muscle injuries sustained during some home renovations and a frantic attempt to get back in shape.

In the course, Ashley began to connect with her body and the ways in which it actually functioned. Posture and movement practices helped her understand how to feel ease in her body. Rest periods during walking short distances and gentle massage or stretching gave her a sense of how the muscles and joints recovered from strain. A deeper practice involved bringing awareness to her heart, lungs, and digestive system so that she could make healthier choices for herself through body awareness. Using the idea of train hopping, Ashley noticed how she ran away from the platform of the body each time it made a demand of her. The trains took her to feelings of anger and frustration, preventing her from seeing what was actually needed in the moment. As her communication skills with her body improved, she spent less and less time going away or avoiding the needs of her body and made healthier choices for herself.

Emotions

On the Emotions platform we experience the full range of our preferences. Love, joy, happiness, loss, sadness, fear, and anger are all part of being on this platform. In the course of therapy, we often ask our patients what emotions they are feeling. It is so interesting to hear responses like: I felt like yelling at her! I felt I was going to explode! I felt like walking out! The answers are about actions and physiological sensations (we'll come to this one in the next section) not about emotions. Most of us have trouble discerning between an emotion and a wish or desire. Our emotional vocabulary tends to be very limited and because of this poverty in communication, we are often surprised that others have a hard time meeting our needs for care and compassion.

Being more mindful of our emotions opens us to what is actually influencing our mental state and what we truly need. Sadness informs us of the need for compassion. Joy allows us to replenish our resources. Anger alerts us to speak and act carefully. Fear protects us from making rash and harmful decisions. When we are available to the language of emotions, our communication with ourselves becomes rich and vibrant even in difficult times.

Kate wanted the "empty mind" that she had read about in books on meditation. She had been practicing for a few years with a local meditation group and was frustrated that she was not experiencing the phenomena other members were talking about. They described experiences of "floating in a sea of bliss" or "being one with all things in the universe." She wanted all that for herself because the waves of emotion she felt were scary and exhausting. She wanted the cocoon of a blank mind so she could feel relief from her inner turmoil.

When she began the meditation practices, she described feeling intense discomfort with the silences. In that spaciousness, she felt vulnerable to everything that surfaced. Sometimes she would have anxiety attacks in the middle of a meditation period. Because of the intensity of the emotions, she tended to switch from one form of meditation to another: breathing to mantra, mantra to chanting, chanting to yoga. Eventually, exhaustion would resolve the problem by forcing her to either stop or fall asleep. When we met Kate, it was of some concern to us that her anxiety attacks may be an obstacle to benefitting from the program. We talked about individual sessions to focus on the anxiety issues but this only seemed to split off one aspect of her experience at the expense of the others. When we explained that she was actually avoiding her true emotional experience and reinforcing the strategy of avoidance by going to a different mode of meditation, she responded with relief. She wasn't incapable of finding that calmness; she had not been listening skillfully to what her emotional nature was trying to tell her. As difficult as it was initially to stay with the uncomfortable emotions, Kate was able to allow the experience of sadness to arise, not engage in stories about the sadness, and watch it subside.

Sensations

Unless we have X-ray vision, we can only know that our various organs are functioning by experiencing the sensations of their functioning. We feel our heart beat, lungs expand, stomach full, chuckling or aching, skin tingling with cold, warmth or even numbness, and so on. There are sensations we may not have thought about as sensations:

- eyes – generate vision sense
- nose – smell sense
- skin – touch sense
- ears – hearing sense
- tongue – taste
- mind – thoughts

These sensations act singly and together as units of data that inform us of the state of our well-being in every moment. When we listen carefully to the messages our body sends to our brain, we are better able to assess that information so that we know what is necessary in the moment. The clarity of our experience allows us to know when we're relaxed, happy, satisfied, hungry, sad, or tired. Knowing our experience and feeling confirmed in it, we are in a better position to meet our needs.

Ed announced to the group that he had no particular reason to attend the sessions other than to explore "stuff." His posture was loose and he projected an attitude of "been there, done that." In fact, he had. His previous experiences with meditation and yoga were with an impressive list of teachers and retreats in places near and far. His professional life was a powerful mix of hard-nosed negotiations in the corporate world and a commitment to social issues. As the course progressed, Ed's reports that everything was just "wonderful" made us more and more curious about what was actually happening in his meditation.

As we inquired into his actual experiences while practicing sitting meditation, he explained that he was aware of his body as a body. In other words, he felt his ankle, his knee, hip bones, and so on. He was aware of his emotions, feelings of calm, bliss, and what he called "being wrapped in a comfortable blanket." At this point, we asked Ed to describe the moments in meditation just before he became aware of those emotions. This surprised him; he believed he had been taught to go past the emotions (yes, joy, label it 'joy' and move on) into this blissful state. So we assigned him a special practice of noticing what he had labeled as a sensation just before he projected himself into that blissful state.

When Ed returned to the next class, he was despondent. He had spent every meditation noticing the aching sensations in his chest. In his view, this was not what meditation was meant to do. As we explored the sequence of his experience, it became clear that as soon as he felt a sensation, particularly the tightness in his chest, he felt distress. His way of dealing with the distress (and the sensation) was to trigger a distance from it. It took a bit of convincing before Ed was willing to stay with the tightness, breathe, and notice how it affected his posture, his mind, and his decisions. He had strong associations between chest-centered sensations and pain, weakness, and even death. As he practiced awareness through the day, he noticed that the tightness was always there and even more prominent when he was about to engage in actions with uncertain consequences or in which he had little conviction. Attending to the sensations and resisting the stories about them, Ed learned that they were not a signal of his weakness or mortality but a powerful warning bell that guided his ethics.

It's worth a note here that the sense of our body (arm, leg, heart, lungs) and the sensations in our body (warm, cold, tingling, pressure) are intricately linked. It is a somewhat arbitrary line in concept but an important one in practice. The line between sensations and emotions is also arbitrary and we'll explore it deeply when we practice on the emotions platform. For now, let's try to work with the concepts of "body", "emotions", "sensations" as we might look at the background, mid-ground and fore-ground of a painting or photograph. All three are present in a unified and inseparable whole but which one we look at is a matter of focus.

Thoughts

Poet Rachel Field wrote of thoughts being like fireflies when we are with some people. Sitting on the deck at our farm on a warm summer evening, we are often treated to a magical display of fairy lights blinking and floating through the trees. As we let our thoughts drift in the comfort of a lazy evening, it almost seems like the thoughts are partners with the fireflies, flitting over us and turning on and off. In moments like that it's hard to believe that something so ephemeral has such power over our ways of being.

Our culture and socialization places a huge emphasis on our thinking capacity. We are evaluated on our ability to perform mental tasks quickly and with clarity. There is much value placed on high levels of intelligence and rational abilities. In fact, emotional states are considered the opposite and less valued because they are seen as "irrational." When our minds are focused and disciplined, the thinking process is a powerful information processing tool and we appropriately can feel satisfied and proud of what we accomplish. It's little wonder that when the mind speaks, we jump to attention believing its message to be absolute fact and very real.

It's easy to see that when our well-being is off balance and our thinking is sluggish or filtered, we become very judgmental (another thinking process) of our abilities and our worth. We treat the loss of concentration, poor memory, distraction, and disjointed associations as something to be feared. While it is possible that these moments are signals of depression, anxiety, or a medical condition, our reaction to them is based on a false belief that our minds are never like this. And, if those beliefs are expressed as thoughts about our worth, we tend to buy them like uninformed consumers.

The mind, however, is a busy place and filled with thoughts that meander and leap-frog over each other. As we may have learned from the exercises above, it doesn't take too many seconds of quiet before the mind is filled with internal chatter. The usual experience though is of a surface process of logical thoughts. ("Oh, I've got to get that sweater from the dryer. I meant to wear it today; the weather looks cool but maybe it will warm up before the meeting's over and I can enjoy that walk to the grocery store before I get home which reminds me, I have to get some dish detergent if we need any, better check to see.") It sounds like we're in charge but there's actually minimal awareness of this mass of competing thoughts or that it plays a role in derailing us.

So, we can start out with the apparently clear intention of going to the laundry room to retrieve a sweater from the dryer and end up in the kitchen looking for dish detergent. We may be driving to work and arrive only to not remember the trip there. We might dial a number on the phone and when the person answers, forget who we were calling. Those blank spaces are only blank in appearance; they are filled with gigabytes of data flowing from brain to body to brain. What we actually express in, or are aware of as thinking, is only the tip of the mind-sense iceberg. It's not surprising then to find ourselves in mood states without knowing how we got there.

Dolores desperately wanted rest from what she called "this radio in my head." She felt bombarded with thoughts and ideas, songs and snippets of conversations. When something would arise in her mind, she felt obliged to follow it up because it "might just be important." Usually, the thoughts were low urgency and were more of a commentary about her surroundings. But once the train got going, it took her everywhere. As she described it, "It's like being on a bus and needing to know where everyone was going and what everyone had done before they got on and what they were going to do when they got off." Sometimes when problem-solving at work, she ended up in twisted rounds of "what-if" and "should-I." She was exhausted from the internal dialogue and debates.

When we described the trains and how we get carried away unaware of where we have been, Dolores lit up. Despite her best efforts, sitting meditation practice was difficult because her thinking habits were strongly taught to pursue and not rest. However, as she practiced with some of the exercises such as the "mindful bell" (described at the end of this chapter), she began to notice spaces between the thoughts. She also began to notice how she tended to encourage the wandering mind because it was her concept of being creative and free. It is certainly the case that a flexible cognitive process results in creativity but we often miss the discipline of that flexibility. As Dolores eventually put it, "There's flexible and then there's getting lost outside the universe. One gets my work done; the other takes me too far away from my work to get it done."

Recovery to Well-Being

The mark of well-being is in the rate of recovery from being off balance. We tend to measure our state of achievement in outcomes: finishing the race or getting a product out on schedule. For the most part, this is necessary. However, when dealing with our physical and mental health, achievement has no meaning. The intention is not so much to finish the race but to ensure that we recover our equilibrium at the finish line. In fact, dying at the finish line is not really considered a success.

Practicing calm awareness in every moment resets our physiology and allows us to access our true nature and the skillfulness that is constantly available to us. In this way we meet the stresses of our daily life with steadiness, keeping our body, emotions, sensations, and thinking in a fitness range and recover in the transparent waters of well-being.

Creating Intention and Continuous Practice

The practice of mindfulness begins with the creation of an intention to pay attention. We suggest using the following practices for at least one week.

Body Scan Use the Body Scan (download or CD) every day. Practice noticing the sensations in your body and practice gentleness in bringing yourself back if you have wandered away from the task. Remember the point is not to have a gripped focus on the body but to just notice what is happening and that includes noticing that you've wandered away. After all, if you don't wander off, you can't get better at practicing your concentration skills. Practice gentleness and notice if you are being harsh or demanding of yourself in the practice.

Mindful Bells Pick a sound or a visual trigger that occurs in some consistent way in your environment. It can be the phone ringing, the picture in the hall, or the walk to the photocopier. Each time the trigger presents itself (the phone rings), bring your attention to your breathing for three in-out breaths. Choose different stimuli each day. Stoplights, brake lights, or turn signals of the car in front of you are all ways to bring yourself back from whatever train you've hopped onto. Attend to your breathing and then resume your work.

There are also computer programs and apps that ring to remind you to return to your breath. A list of these can be found in the Resource chapter at the end of the book.

Daily awareness Choose a specific task you do each day such as brushing your teeth, showering, combing you hair, drinking your coffee or tea. Bring your full attention to the task feeling all the sensations in that moment.

Fill in the Practice Record Sheet Use the sheet to record the mindful bells you choose and the times you practiced the Body Scan. These are good ways to create intention and build credits in your training of skillful habits. Feel free to reward yourself (mindfully!) when you've realized your aspirations to nurture well-being.

Record of Daily Practice – Week 1

Note each time you have practiced the Body Scan or the "bells of mindfulness." Write your observations about each experience.

Day/Date	Body Scan	Bell of Mindfulness	Observations
Day 1 Date:	Y N	Type:	
Day 2 Date:	Y N	Type:	
Day 3 Date:	Y N	Type:	
Day 4 Date:	Y N	Type:	
Day 5 Date:	Y N	Type:	
Day 6 Date:	Y N	Type:	
Day 7 Date:	Y N	Type:	

Lynette Monteiro, Frank Musten

CHAPTER 2:
Meeting the Difficult and the Unwanted

Our intention in this chapter: *The beginning of every practice is both energizing and frustrating. Let's look at what comes from intentionally noticing our experience in these early days of training our attention.*

The Experience of Noticing

The Body Scan is our first introduction to hearing the voice of the body just as it is in this moment. When we lie down (or sit up) and have brought our awareness to each part of the body, we may have experienced a variety of physical and emotional sensations. Meet some of our friends on this path:

Jason, the lawyer in the last chapter who was diagnosed with an autoimmune disease, described feeling exhausted and falling asleep each time he did the Body Scan. He began to dread the exercises.

Bob couldn't find the time to do the exercises and forgot about it most of the week. He felt guilt and worry about coming to the class and facing what he believed would be our disappointment.

Ashley noticed that her body was in far more pain than she had thought it was. She was not happy that something intended to make her feel better was "backfiring."

Tim insisted that it was the answer to all his problems because he felt relaxed. He was quite happy with this.

Joe realized that the sensations could be very demanding and confusing – the ache in his back dragged attention away from his foot but disappeared when it was time to bring attention to it.

Laura hated the whole exercise because to her it was more proof that she couldn't do anything right. She felt angry and dove into her usual strategy of wanting to know what to expect so she could "calibrate her performance."

When the experience of trying to do the exercises or the experience during the exercises is not what we expect, we believe we've hit a roadblock. We make assumptions about the difficulties and may feel that we are not going to get any benefits from the practice. The fatigue, lack of time, or painful sensation becomes an obstacle that adds one more layer of struggle to our quest for well-being. When we meet these obstacles in our path by pushing them away or clinging to old "tried and true" strategies, we prevent ourselves from continuing or developing a different attitude about well-being.

Let's look at what some of these experiences are and how we can change our relationship with them.

What is the True Nature of the Roadblocks

Time

The most common experience of a roadblock is the lack of time to do the Body Scan. We all have days overflowing with things that take our attention away from our good intentions to cultivate well-being. From the moment we wake up until we close our eyes at night, it seems we are on the go meeting everyone's demands. Making breakfast and lunches, driving kids or partners to work, meetings all day, volunteering our time for others, caring for aging parents, getting kids to their activities, helping with home-work, making dinner –the list goes on and on. Adding 30-45 minutes of lying down (and apparently doing nothing!) seems hard to justify in the face of everyone else's agenda and our sense of urgency.

If we take a close look, time is not really the problem. However, our relationship to time can be. The attitude we take to those 30 or 45 minutes is the real obstacle to our practice. When we see the 30 minutes of medita-tion as taking something away from someone or something else, we set up the roadblock to setting out on this journey of well-being.

Space

The second experience we have in trying to do these exercises is finding a quiet space. Compared to most of the world, our living conditions are luxurious yet we seem to have tremendous difficulty finding a space in which we can just lie down. Add in our time demands and the likelihood of a conjunction of space and an uninterrupted period of time seems unlikely.

Like time, our perception of space is affected by our relationship to it. We create an image of a sanctuary with intense quiet and soothing visuals: a fountain, candles, dark hardwood floors, or flowers perfectly arranged. Here we can meditate endlessly without the phone ringing or the children pounding up the stairs. The world disappears and we find nirvana. If beautiful spaces were the only factor of enlightenment, sunsets would bring us all into well-being instantly and permanently.

What is

The third experience is the experience itself – and the doubt about it that follows. We are creatures of dreams and desires. When we hurt we desire the end of hurting. When hurting is large and fills our horizon, we feel blinded by the suffering. We desire more strongly an end to this suffering and will grasp for anything that appears to promise it can shrink the pain. And here we are, lying down, pretending not to hope that this simple act of bringing attention to our toes, feet, legs, abdomen, back, chest, arms, face, and head is going to do what no other intervention has done: free us from suffering.

Instead we encounter the reality of our suffering. We discover that it is here, now, and has us in its grip. Every sensation we have ignored or misinterpreted is now totally available to us and sometimes at full volume. If we have been dealing with chronic pain, our sensations may seem like they've intensified. If we are struggling with depression, we may wonder how the heck paying attention to our toes is going to make a difference in feeling better and reduce the likelihood of becoming depressed again. Anxious feelings may arise as we wonder if we're doing things the 'right' way when we aren't feeling any better after the first or second practice session.

Sometimes we may feel so frustrated we go back to old habits or practices. Disappointment is inevitable when we begin any activity; the doubt that arises is also a normal process. These are not the real diversions in our practice. The real roadblock is in believing that doubt means we should just return to the "tried and true."

Knowing

The fourth and perhaps the biggest challenges to practice are the realizations that the experience opens in us. When Jason discovered during each Body Scan that he was fatigued, it was his first understanding of how depleted his resources were. In class, he described the anxiety that arose initially, as he had to come to terms with the effects of trying to meet unrelenting demands at work and home. He wondered if he wasn't just better off not knowing and then realized it was now – and perhaps best that it was - too late. He had to make changes in his life or face more serious health consequences.

Ashley's awareness of her pain was a shock to her. She had always worked on the principle that knowing less was better for her because it allowed her to cope. Now she had to confront the fallacy that ignorance is bliss and begin to listen carefully to her body's signals about her real limits.

Our body's messages about our true state cannot be blocked forever. Listening carefully however requires openness to what the message means about our past and future choices. Feeling the fatigue means our plans may need to be re-considered or re-designed. Feeling pain means our concepts of pacing may require re-training. Activities may have to be postponed or set aside. Ideas may have to be re-configured. Minds may have to change. As with time, space and knowing, the true nature of our experience is not the event that was difficult or the experience that was unwanted. The real obstacle to well-being is that we believe the presence of the difficult and unwanted means something negative about us.

One particular realization is that we cannot always accomplish everything exactly the way we had planned. The guilt that arises from that observation is the most common experience at this stage of the practice. We feel guilt when we aren't finding the time to practice. We feel guilt when we do manage to wrench the time away from family and work to practice. And, if we're especially hard on ourselves, shame accompanies guilt just to juice things up.

Is there a way around these obstacles? How do we meet these

roadblocks and use them wisely?

Opening the Path

Although paying attention seems initially to just complicate our lives, we slowly begin to notice not only the unpleasant experiences but also the pleasant and neutral ones. Our vision expands to include all aspects of our sensory world. Remember that when we practiced the awareness of senses exercise in the previous chapter, we noticed the many different sensations by which we could experience the dried fruit. Similarly, when we expand our attention each time we encounter an event in our life, we give ourselves more options for skillful action.

When Jason worked with the Body Scan, he began to notice there was more than just fatigue that was present. In the first few moments of the Body Scan, he felt his whole body was a dead weight pressing into the floor. As soon as he felt this he noticed how his mind created stories about how awful it was to feel so tired. In the first few sessions of practice, much of his time was spent unlatching himself from these stories and trains to nowhere. As he progressed through the various parts of the body, he began to notice that his neck and upper back were tense however his arms felt light. His breath began as tight and controlled but slowly shifted into long, slow inhalations and exhalations. On some days, he could identify his sensations as fatigue; on other days he sensed more of a loosening of tension than fatigue. Over time, Jason began to re-define the sensations and not get on as many trains away from his experience. As he put it in class, "It's feels like it would be easier to run away on a train about what it all means than to just feel the sensations. But it's actually more useful to know that what I'm feeling is really just muscle sensations and not necessarily fatigue."

Bob began to notice how his tendency to put everyone's needs ahead of himself were really the cause of his anger and frustration. He struggled with finding time and took a non-judgmental attitude when he couldn't. Instead of labeling himself a failure when he didn't take the 30 or 40 minutes to practice, he used the mindful bells as his little "oasis" in his busy days.

Ashley tried to meet her pain with openness each time she lay down. She still found herself emotionally reactive to the cycles of pain and relief;

she noticed she was cycling by pushing away the pain and then trying to hold onto the relief. Over time she noticed that the tightening and letting go were phases that she could ride with rather than force her way through.

Tim was just happy he had found something that worked. He felt relaxed and that was his main objective. It is important to understand that the purpose of the Body Scan is not to feel relaxed. It is training to notice the entire fabric of our experience. The gold threads and the tears in the fabric are equally valued and observed without preference. When we can adopt a non-preferential stance to whatever shows up on our horizon, we develop a steadiness and a lowered tendency to get carried away on those trains. However, for Tim, the side effect of relaxation was a good starting point.

Joe began to notice the workings of the mind. As he watched the way in which it clung to one sensation and then another, he began to understand the monkey mind. He also noticed that he was very harsh with himself when his mind flitted and flew all over his internal landscape. His words were judgmental and sometimes cruel. Joe was surprised by the language in his head and the automaticity of his reactions to his perceived failures. He reported that practicing a gentle return to the body was more kindness than he ever thought he deserved.

Laura, like Joe, began to uncover the underlying harshness in her attitude to herself. For her however, all the practices were a sign that she was in fact worthless or stupid. She couldn't remember to do the mindful bells, the Body Scan only created severe agitation, and the daily activities were lost in the tumble of self-derogatory comments. Working with her inner critic was a challenge and she was unconvinced that even just noticing the harshness was a good beginning. We'll meet up with Laura later in our journey.

Let's put this in the CARR formula we learned in the last chapter: Calm, Aware, Remember, Recover. As we calm body and mind through the practices like the Body Scan, we become more aware of the many layers of our experience. What is initially an obstacle can be seen as an attitude or a judgment of the experience itself. Slowly we begin to remember our intention is to learn how to separate our judgments about an experience from the actual experience. As we disengage from our harsh relationship with our body and mind, we recover through a skillful cultivation of well-being.

Cultivating Well-Being through Skillful Effort

Practicing mindfulness skills such as the Body Scan is a first step to learning how to stop struggling with the difficult and the unwanted. By creating the space and time to be aware of how our body is communicating with us through physical/emotional sensations and thoughts, we are cultivating steadiness in the face of anything we may experience. Our increasing awareness exposes the massive effort we put into pushing away our experience or clinging to past experiences as a measure of our performance.

In that sense, we're no stranger to effort. In fact, we put in so much effort in getting things done "perfectly" for ourselves and everyone else that it's a shock to see how unskillful we can be at the simple act of lying down and observing. Often police officers and firefighters who take the 8-week course comment that they would much rather be in life-threatening situations than lie down with the Body Scan! This is not unusual because we always associate effort with a tangible outcome against which we can measure our value.

Skillful effort on the other hand requires something very different. It is the application of just the amount of energy to meet the demand of the moment. No more, no less. So let's explore how we can develop our capacity for sustaining well-being through the right kind of effort.

Feeding What is Not Beneficial

The first type of effort is to stop practicing the non-beneficial actions. Clearing time and space, noticing the wandering mind, getting off emotional train rides, and letting go of doubt all consume the early stages of cultivating well-being. Think of this phase as managing the clutter or clearing out the weeds in the landscape. There are many habits we have cultivated in our negligence of where and how our minds wander. It's not surprising that when we start paying attention, we are greeted with this tangled mess of attentional habits!

Behavioral habits tend to be well-trained actions that are automatic: the many cups of coffee in a day to keep our energy up, the late nights to meet expectations of work and family, unending hours in front of the TV trying to relax, fast foods, smoking, drinking too much, and so on. They tend to be massive (and therefore unskillful) efforts to manage the demands in our life. It's not realistic to think we can rid ourselves permanently of these ways that we use to deal with our stress. The more skillful approach is to begin to notice the effects of these actions. As we increase our awareness of the impact of these autopilot behaviours, we can begin to adjust and shift our behaviours in a way that reduces the negative impact on our lives.

Behavioral observations are at the easier end of the spectrum of creating change. They tend to be tangible things we do and so we can imagine doing something different. Other habits are less tangible.

Our deeply ingrained ways of thinking are also automatic: self-derogatory comments, angry internal outbursts, self-blame, guilt. They lie in wait ready to be triggered by some action that we assess as lacking in perfection. Thinking patterns are a wonderful opportunity to examine more closely how we buy into the subtle or not-so-subtle stories about our unworthiness. Stopping them however is a challenge because of their ephemeral nature. A good start is the gentle return to the breath during the mindful bells or the non-judgmental guidance back to the body during the Body Scan.

We talked about guilt earlier in this chapter. Let's look at that closely. Guilt is often a measure between who we had hoped to be and who we actually are in the moment. It exposes how we believe we have fallen short of our target. Depending on our life experiences, we may end up using it as a huge stick to punish ourselves or beat us into greater effort.

> *Notice the overt behaviours that lead to non-beneficial outcomes.*
> *Don't encourage them.*
> *Notice the subtle thinking patterns that lead to negativity.*
> *Don't encourage them.*

Sometimes, guilt is a way of avoiding being judged by others. If we commit to doing the mindfulness exercises and don't, then a show of guilt – or even excessive guilt – is a protection against someone telling us we disappointed them. As one participant said with insight, "No one's going to join me in the bash-fest if I'm already beating myself up!" For most of us, guilt, shame, and self-recrimination are excessive ways of teaching us how to avoid behaviours that are harmful to ourselves and others. Unfortunately this strategy tends to backfire severely by just reinforcing our wrong belief about self-worth.

Return to our acronym, CARR, for practice from the last chapter: Calm, Aware, Remember, Recover. By practicing gentleness when we fall short of our mark, we calm our reactivity to our perceptions of poor performance. As we become aware of our behavioral and thinking habits, we begin to shift the thinking habits away from the self-destructive tendencies. We can then remember our intentions and return to (recover) the supportive behaviours or thoughts that can help us sustain that shift.

Nurture What is Beneficial

The second type of effort is the cultivation of useful and beneficial habits. A long time ago, Lynette used to work with families who had trouble managing their child's negative behaviours. They would have a litany of all the things their child would do that ranged from disruptive to dangerous. Sometimes these children would be prescribed medication to increase attention and reduce the intensity of the negative interactions in the family and in school. Interestingly, parents would then report that even though attention had increased and their child was no longer hitting, biting, kicking or generally having difficulty with others, positive behaviours were not surfacing. In fact, parental reports of increased pleasantness in their relationship with their child were based on the absence of unpleasantness. Parents also seemed to anticipate that pleasant behaviours would spontaneously surface when the unpleasant behaviours were managed. It was always a surprise to the parents to learn that the unpleasant behaviours were not masking or suppressing the pleasant ones.

Beneficial behaviours need to be cultivated. In childhood, we are encouraged to be polite, generous, and kind. In adulthood, we strive to continue these lessons from childhood and, human failings aside, we manage quite well to be giving and gentle with our friends and family. However, for the most part we don't extend that same gentleness to ourselves. Let's visit with Laura for a while to see how this unfolds in her life.

Laura had grown in a family environment that was harsh and critical. Everything she did was scrutinized for imperfections. Even when there were compliments, there was always a hint of not having been good enough. Laura internalized these negative and ambiguous evaluations as an accurate reflection of her own unworthiness. In the class when we read Mary Oliver's poem Wild Geese, Laura reacted intensely to the first line of the poem which invites us to take a different stance to our internal critic; it suggests we "do not have to be good." She struggled with the invitation to see ourselves in a different light, to have a different relationship with our striving. More than that, she began to touch the harsh punitive ways in which she dealt with her striving. Every action was filled with the potential for failure and any success was a threat because it meant it would raise the bar of expectations. She was stuck in a very painful space of wanting to achieve but being afraid to invest in the achievement.

Doing the Body Scan, Laura began to notice that she was not only encouraging the old negative habits but had no model for noticing the quiet signs of success. So, we worked on congratulating her for noticing – just noticing. It was not easy because whatever she noticed was tightly fused to the automatic self-berating. We worked on noticing that too and praising her for noticing it. Laura would argue and complain that the techniques were not working. We encouraged her to notice that she was putting in the effort. Laura wanted to give up. We encouraged her to notice that she had come to the class on that day. Laura asked if everyone else was having the same problems. We encouraged her to notice how she sought community when she was uncertain. Laura said we couldn't possibly know how she felt. We encouraged her to see that she was able to trust her own feelings. Laura accused us of encouraging sloppiness by settling for less than 100% perfection. We encouraged her to value whatever percentage of perfection she had achieved as a good starting point for today.

> *Read the poem "Wild Geese" by*
> *Mary Oliver*
>
> *What does "being good" mean for*
> *you? What does it mean to belong in*
> *the family of things?*

Wild Geese[3]

You do not have to be good.
You do not have to walk on your knees
for a hundred miles through the desert, repenting.
You only have to let the soft animal of your body
        love what it loves.
Tell me about despair, yours, and I will tell you mine.
Meanwhile the world goes on.
Meanwhile the sun and the clear pebbles of the rain
are moving across the landscapes,
over the prairies and the deep trees,
the mountains and the rivers.
Meanwhile the wild geese, high in the clean blue air,
are heading home again.
Whoever you are, no matter how lonely,
the world offers itself to your imagination,
calls to you like the wild geese, harsh and exciting—
over and over announcing your place
in the family of things.

For Laura and many others, self-nurturing is an alien concept so a lot of time is needed to encourage self-care and nourish the internal – but deeply buried – wellness. Laura came to every class; she did every home practice we offered. These were wonderful seeds to nurture and nourish. Her frustration was based on her expectations of a particular outcome and she judged herself not on her effort but on those outcomes.

> *What seeds were planted that have not been nurtured in you?*
>
> *What seeds have blossomed that need to be nourished?*

As is typical of the constellation of high expectations and hyper-vigilance of wrong-doing, guilt and shame followed them as close companions. Guilt can, in fact, be a useful mindful bell that wakes us up to the possibility of

---

3   From Mary Oliver, *Dream Work*. Copyright© 1986 by Mary Oliver. Reprinted by permission of Grove Atlantic, Inc.

doing things differently. A skillful use of guilt can lead us to see what we did accomplish rather than become blinded by our striving.

The 100% Trap

Most of us judge ourselves by the difference between the outcome of our actions and what we had hoped the outcome would be. We tend to ignore factors like effort or human limitations and cultivate a self-perception that is out-of-balance. Like Laura we fear that accepting less than 100% perfection is a cop-out or a reflection of poor values. It's a trap in which our every decision becomes fear-based and fear-driven.

One of our teachers used to caution against this need for 100% perfection in our interactions as a teacher of mindfulness. She would say that when people are asking for a drink of water to quench their suffering from thirst, a little sip is better than hosing them down. We often noticed that when we strove for perfection as teachers, we tended to give more information than someone could process in that moment. The message was often more effective when the dose of our responses met the need of the person in front of us – even if the dose-related response was only about half of what we thought was the "best" response.

If we start with a view that 30 or 40 or 80% is just what is necessary in this moment, we release our death-grip on having to achieve our ideal goal right now. We begin to notice the freedom it gives to explore ways to encourage ourselves. For a while those pesky trains about perfection can seem to rule our lives. As we practice, we begin to notice sooner that we are being carried away in fear and how that fear actually prevents skillfulness in our efforts. As we learn to be steady and calm in the knowledge that we have wandered from our core intention, we can see the way to return to that core and generate the means to meet our goals in a healthy way.

The North Star

Zen master Thich Nhat Hanh encourages us to use our ideals as we would use the North Star to navigate our journey. With gentle humor he points out that the North Star is indispensible to finding our way around the obstacles and courses of our life. But the intention is neither to get to the

North Star nor to live there. The intention is to live well in the internal territory of our body and mind as well as the external landscape of our lives.

We aspire to live well and sustain well-being in every moment. When we notice the stories about our unworthiness and let go of them, we begin to chart the first leg of our journey. As we expand our awareness of the whole range of our experience (pleasant, unpleasant, and neutral), we see that our territory is not just this depression, anxiety, physical pain or other illness. It is, and therefore we are, much larger and more interesting.

Skillful effort is exerting just what force is required to meet what is in this moment.
No need to push or pull!

Continuing Your Practice

Body Scan Do the Body Scan 6 times this week. Notice the breath as it moves through your body. Notice the changes in the breath as you approach areas of tension or concern.

Breathing meditation Sit in a quiet place and follow the breath. Notice the In breath and the Out breath: the texture, temperature, flow. Do it 6 times this week for 3 minutes each. Use the breath to steady yourself in situations, to notice when you are caught in a story, to bring yourself to "what is".

Mindful Bells Continue to practice with various stimuli in your environment to bring you back to the breath.

Pleasant Experiences Complete the table of Pleasant Experiences (Appendix A). Notice what it is about the event that you feel is pleasant. What does your body feel like? What thoughts did you have? How are the judgmental thoughts infusing the event? The purpose of this exercise is to bring awareness to the things we actually experience as pleasant (we tend to miss them). It is also a way of "saving" them to the "hard drive" of our neural network so that the body has a memory of what "pleasant" feels like.

Skillful Effort Pay attention to how you are exerting yourself. What was your intention? Write it down. What does this event need in this moment? Write it down. What is possible? Write it down.

Record of Daily Practice – Week 2

Note each time you have practiced the Body Scan or the "bells of mindfulness". Write your observations about each experience.

Day/Date	Body Scan	Bell of Mindfulness	Observations
Day 1 Date:	Y N	Type:	
Day 2 Date:	Y N	Type:	
Day 3 Date:	Y N	Type:	
Day 4 Date:	Y N	Type:	
Day 5 Date:	Y N	Type:	
Day 6 Date:	Y N	Type:	
Day 7 Date:	Y N	Type:	

CHAPTER 3:
Awareness of the Body

Our intention in this chapter: *Our body is the container and source of all our experiences. We have functioned not only from the belief that the body operates separately from the mind but that the mind is the sole determinant of our wisdom. A practice of mindfulness of the body begins with re-membering ourselves, bringing our awareness back into the body, of the body, and to partnership with the body.*

Awareness of the Body

While doing the Body Scan every day, we begin to notice aspects of our body we may have taken for granted. The aches and pains, the tension, the soreness may have all taken a back seat as we try to negotiate through our days. And then simply by lying still and listening, we begin to hear the many ways in which the body communicates its ease and dis-ease. It's not uncommon to hear participants in the courses talk about discovering parts of their body they never thought had sensations, feeling the sensation of their heart beating or lungs expanding. It's also very common to hear participants who struggle with chronic pain express their distress that their experience of pain increases or that they weren't aware of how fatigued they were. In fact, awareness of fatigue (and falling asleep during the Body Scan) is a typical reaction of almost all participants!

For the most part we tend to live outside our bodies. More accurately, we live up in our heads and consider the body not much more than a vehicle for getting the mind from place to place. While that may be a useful concept, it's not a very beneficial one. It often amazes us that we tend to make more of and take better care of our cars than we do of this container of our experience. And perhaps, that's the flaw in our thinking. We view the body only as a container rather than a massively complex communication device which integrates information at the interface of our inner and outer environment.

Another concept worth exploring is the assumption that this particular body was specifically designed to fulfill our dreams and desires. We are immersed in messages that we can do anything if we only set our minds to it. The subtext is that the body will cooperate with whatever the mind designs. There are certainly many bodies that can become whatever the mind desires. Athletes, firefighters, police officers, military members, and so on can and do train their bodies to be specifically designed to meet certain needs. Even so, every one of us has to eventually face the inevitability of our body's limits and deterioration.

Awareness of Breath & the Four Platforms of Mindfulness

We connect with our body through mindfulness using two main practices from Buddhist psychology: *Awareness of Breath* and *Four Platforms of Mindfulness* . These next four chapters in this book focus on the framework of the Four Platforms of Mindfulness (Body, Feelings, Mind, and what arises from Mind) and in each platform we practice with the breath as a conditioner of the body, emotions, sensations, and thoughts. This grid of practices forms the template through which we process our experiences, by which we navigate to refine the skillfulness of our choices.

This Body Mine

Let's begin by developing awareness of our body.

Our bodies are fragile. At birth we require a lot of care and protection to survive. As infants, we are dependent on others for our feeding, cleaning, and being protected. We develop individual strategies to deal with our physical nature as we mature. Depending on what was valued in our developmental years, we may pursue active or sedentary physical lifestyles. We may develop good or poor eating habits. We may be prone or resistant to disease. In fact, it's somewhat amazing that we survive at all given the myriad of possibilities that impact on our physical nature.

The flip side then is that our bodies are also resilient. Lack of sleep, poor nutrition, excessive stress, fast pace; whatever we do to it, the body seems to recover enough to keep going. We survive accidents, illnesses, and distress. Bones mend, hearts are repaired, minds come back into balance. Because we seem to cope so well with the strain we place on our body, we think of it (if we think of it at all) as being impervious to whatever assaults it. For the most part, we tend to engage the body in activities and give little thought to its need for rest and regeneration. Why then are we shocked and dismayed when the body says, "Enough! If you won't let me rest, I will take charge of stopping without consensus or cooperation."

We may rest but it is rarely sufficient for physical regeneration and we associate slowing down or taking breaks as signs of weakness, lack of dedication, or not measuring up. It doesn't help matters when we hold in high esteem those who can push their bodies beyond normal limits. Athletes who challenge their bodies to climb mountains, scale cliffs, and endure marathons earn our admiration easily. We are in awe of people who draw on unimaginable physical resources to survive hardships like war, famine, capture, and torture. And, when we can't keep up to those standards, we feel ashamed of ourselves. Our body, which may not be as resilient as we assume, then becomes a battleground between our self-respect and what it means to have limitations.

Susan was unwilling to accept that she needed time off from work to recover from the strain of caring for her dying parent. She repeated her mantra often: Other people have it worse. If anyone tried to point out the huge load she was carrying, she insisted that someone with a strong work ethic and who was dedicated to their family would be able to do it all. Her daily routine was unforgiving: She woke up at 4:30 a.m. every morning to prepare breakfast and lunch for her parent and to get ready to go to work. Starting work at 7:30 a.m. allowed her to leave early and be home for the evening care. Sometimes, at noon, she would go home to check on things. Even if she managed to get home by 4 p.m. she rarely had a chance to rest before diving into the next round of chores. After dinner and washing up, she'd fall asleep on the sofa only to find herself unable to sleep through the night. She felt anxious and dreaded the next day.

Jason and Ashley had similar attitudes to their bodies. They both believed that if they committed to ensuring they were fit and healthy, they would be spared illness. Jason exercised religiously and was determined to manage his high stress levels that way. Ashley focused on eating good foods that helped manage her weight and allowed her to feel good about herself. Neither had inappropriate expectations of themselves given they were in good physical health and derived great pleasure out of their highly driven lifestyles. And neither expected to suffer the physical challenges of an auto-immune disease or an injury; nor did they expect their bodies not to blow through the illness or injury as it had with all other physical challenges.

Like most people under stress, Susan, Jason, and Ashley blamed them-selves for the non-physical symptoms. Difficulty concentrating, poor memory, irritability, and loss of interest in activities were all seen as an inability to be strong and competent. At the same time, fatigue, aches and pains, headaches, and weight gain were seen as their body's refusal to coop-erate to get things done. Their inner critic had a field day anytime the body tried to communicate its needs or the mind tried to slow things down.

Strain and Stress

Canadian researcher Hans Selye (1907-1982) developed a theory of stress that described the body's reaction to events. Physiologically, the body responds and adapts to the strain that events place on it. Interestingly, these events don't have to be negative. The adaptation process is the same whether the event has positive or negative implications. We brace ourselves for change and then adapt to that change. When change is unre-lenting to the point of being chaotic, we no longer adapt. We collapse. Psychologically, we cope with the process of strain by developing strate-gies that may not result in helpful consequences (we'll explore this further in Chapter 6).

As we learned in the previous chapter, it's not the actual event that causes us distress; it's how we relate to the event. Illness and injury happen to everybody at one point or another. We know we aren't really going to escape it, but in order to cope we tend to keep that knowledge well in the background of our awareness. To aid in our self-protection, we develop concepts of our body that are useful in getting us through the life we have. These concepts foster the idea of a physical system that can mobilize to meet any challenge.

Let's walk with our bodies through a regular day. It likely begins with a clanging wakeup call sometime between 4 and 6 a.m. All systems are shocked into consciousness even if it doesn't feel like it. As we gain the surface of awareness, we probably feel sluggish, groggy and thoughts like, "Ugh, already? But I just fell asleep!" or "Why am I so lazy?" slip through and build our self-concept. Beneath that thinking layer, the nervous system is activated and firing like crazy. In fact, the stress hormone, cortisol, which normally increases through the latter half of the night's sleep, increases by an average of 50% just after awakening. It is suggested that this increase is the body's way of mobilizing for stress. And look, we haven't even got out of bed yet!

Now let's continue with our day: going to the toilet, brushing teeth, showering, breakfast, and preparing for the day. The body seems quite cooperative and gets itself through all these tasks. It would be hard to imagine ourselves as frail and fragile (unless we've already hit that reality through illness or injury). Then we get to the daily commute to work or other chores that bring us into contact with a world of intense demands. Driving to work is rarely a stress-free event and a good place to begin to notice how we inadvertently lay the groundwork for the body's vulnerability to stress.

Depending on the length and intensity of our commute, by the time we hit the office entrance, we've likely been practicing a range of stress-triggering behaviours such as teeth clenching, back muscle tightening, eyes narrowing, and shoulder hunching. The phone's message alert is likely blinking as may be the email notifications. Colleagues wander in with demands before greetings. We probably become aware in the first few minutes that lunch is not about to happen nor is supper. In a flash, we're already at the end of our day, exhausted and wishing it was bedtime!

Through the day, there has been little or no time to reset the physiology that began the day at high alert. At the end of the day,

When you completed the table of events you experienced as pleasant, what did you notice?

Were they events, moments that you normally would have noticed? What sensations did you notice in your body during the event? As you recall the event now?

we feel like we've survived. Although we have, it's been at a cost that is not immediately tangible. In our classes, we refer to the cost as the "Phantom Withdrawal" from our "Resilience Bank Account". Because we don't tend to replenish the bank account, it runs low without our awareness. As we wear down, we begin to mistake surviving the day for having met the day well. When these two lines, using up resources and not refilling the tank, converge, our bodies cave in. Add physical illness or injury to the mix and it becomes explosive.

Therefore, it's little wonder that when we do stop and still our forward plunge into dis-ease, the body revolts by contracting into itself. If this is our "usual" day, it should come as no surprise when there is no resilience to buffer the fall. To increase our skillfulness in caring for this body, we must begin to take a different stance to it. In the words of Joan Halifax, author of *Being with Dying* , we need to cultivate a soft front and a strong back. The soft front opens us to the possibilities in our life as it is and the strong back allows us to be transparent to what is unfolding for us in this very moment.

Breath Conditions Body

Practicing the Body Scan has given us an opportunity to observe the breath flow in and out of the body. It has also shown us that the rhythm of our breath has an impact on the body. Often, participants in mindfulness programs report feeling more relaxed and having a sense of well-being at the end of the Body Scan. Although that's not the intention of the exercise, it does tell us that a slow, steady breathing rhythm produces changes in the body.

We know, for example, that hyperventilation leads to changes in the amount of carbon dioxide in the blood which causes the brain blood cells to constrict. The lightheadedness that follows can lead to discomfort or fainting. This is probably the most powerful evidence we have of the impact the breath has on the body. In 1971, Harvard University professor Herbert Benson discovered that eliciting the body's ability to relax naturally counteracted its other natural tendency of fight-or-flight. Using breathing techniques, he discovered the heart and respiratory rates decreased and there was a feeling of deep rest. What Benson was able to show was that two competing responses (fight/flight and relaxation) could not exist together in our system. More than that, he showed that practicing with the breath strengthened the relaxation response so that flight-or-flight did not become the default or reactive mode of responding.

> Sit for a minute and bring your attention to your breathing. What happens in your body as you attend to your breath?

As we proceed through the chapters, we will practice bringing an awareness of breathing to our activities. Beginning with the body, as we have by practicing the Body Scan, we can start to re-condition our physical response (and later emotional and other responses) to be less reactive or steadier in the presence of distress.

Five Skillful Habits: Practicing What We Value

An interconnected intention of a mindfulness practice is to cultivate stewardship of our body, mind, and actions with respect to our relationships and environment. Our intentions are best realized when they have a framework that guides their realization. When we re-connect with who we are, we re-orient ourselves in our internal landscape. It has been our experience that navigation is greatly assisted by the use of a North Star. Call it what you will - magnetic fields, GPS, or simple foldout maps – we all need a directional guide for our intentions. Mindfulness is the practice of seeing clearly so that our options are evident. Once those options are evident, we can explore how to take the path that is most congruent with our intention to live well. To cultivate our stewardship of body, speech and action, we have developed Five Skillful Habits to practice throughout the course. By incorporating them into the program we hope to ground our practice in a solid framework that will guide us through the choppy waters of making life choices.

Our practices in skillful living that we shared earlier set our roots firmly in an ethical framework of practice. Buddhist practitioners live by five precepts: do not kill, do not steal, do not commit sexual misconduct, do not lie, and do not us intoxicants. The intention of these precepts is to keep the mind clear and the compass set towards living skillfully. These precepts were reformulated by Thich Nhat Hanh as a creative offering to mindfulness practitioners which can be practiced regardless of religious denomination or secular persuasion. More importantly, his interpretation of the precepts as Five Mindfulness Trainings with which we can engage is crucial because they move away from a prohibition (e.g., do not do X). They offer an opportunity to pay attention to our actions and create the intention to practice an everyday behavioral skill.

From the principles of the Five Mindfulness Trainings, we have derived Five Skillful Habits:

1. Aware of our own suffering and that of others, we practice in ways that cultivate **respect for the preciousness of our life** . Behavioral examples of this habit might be accessing appropriate treatments, taking medication that may be necessary to manage mood or physiology, monitoring blood pressure and nutritional intake, or being aware of thoughts that increase the potential for self-harm.

2. Aware of our own needs and those of others, we practice ways to be **generous** that are sustaining and not depleting. Behaviours that cultivate this habit can include getting rest, acceptance of emotional states, self-compassion during moments of painful physical or emotional sensations, and developing curiosity about the nature of our experience.

3. Aware of the damage done by a violation of boundaries (sexual, physical, emotional), we practice ways to **respect our sexual, physical, and emotional boundaries** that strengthen our self-worth. Behaviours reflecting this habit include setting physical and emotional boundaries with others, playing compassionately with the edges of our own physical tolerance, and cultivating awareness of the mind states that take us to the edge of our boundaries.

4. Aware of the hurt caused by thoughtless and harsh speech, we practice ways to **speak with mindfulness** so that we feel encouraged, supported, and trusted in our internal and external speech. Behaviours to practice can include gentle inner and outer speech about our physical and emotional state.

5. Aware of waste and its destructive consequences as well as liv-

ing in toxic internal and external environments, we practice ways to **consume mindfully** so that we foster well-being in ourselves and our communities. Behaviours to cultivate this habit involve being careful of the things to which we expose ourselves: internal and external toxic environments, nutritional choices, angry interchanges, and images of violence.

To cultivate these five habits, we bring our attention to an aspect of our practice (body, emotions, sensations, and thinking) and define our intention as a specific behaviour (or behaviours) to be practiced with an attitude of openness and curiosity. For us, these Five Skillful Habits are the pillars on which the program is seated and the beating heart of a mindfulness practice.

Cultivating Compassionate Awareness of Our Body through the Five Skillful Habits

Let's take some time to explore how we will apply the Five Skillful Habits to being more caring about our body. Each week we will be applying this approach to cultivate compassionate awareness of our emotions, sensations, and thoughts. We tend to have a roller coaster relationship with our bodies. When things are going well, we derive great pleasure from the power of being well and fit. However, we also take it for granted that the body will take care of itself and always be available on command. The Five Skillful Habits may not ensure that readiness but they will help us build resilience to the inevitable change we all encounter whether it is the predictable ones of aging or the unpredictable ones of illness.

Respecting our mortality is not something we usually keep in the forefront of our mind. Accepting the reality of our mortality however can free us from acting out in ways that deny our limited lifespan. Since the real issue is that we are living and dying simultaneously - every one of us with no exceptions. The question is whether we are living skillfully as we die or dying unskillfully as we live. One of the key practices in Buddhism is the recollection of five features of our humanity:

- We grow old
- We die
- We become ill
- We lose all those we love in one way or another
- We have only our actions as our legacy

It can seem depressing at first glance to think that the richness of our life, its potential for a greater purpose, its profound interconnections, can be reduced mercilessly to these five realities. Yet if we don't acknowledge the essence of the physical nature of our life, at least in the first three realities, we are operating from a biased perspective.

Looking at these realities through a different lens, we can see the deeper teachings. We can see that there is no need to waste time on frivolously maintaining youth. It would be better to do the things that allow the aging physique to adapt well to its impermanence. Many participants in mindfulness programs discover activities like martial arts, yoga, and tai chi keep the body flexible and they develop a deeper awareness of their physical strengths and vulnerabilities.

How are you practicing adaptability? There is nothing more certain than death and taxes. Grumble though we might, we end up paying the taxes just as inevitably as we will meet that last good night. The choice is not whether we die well but whether we live practicing resentment that our life has a "best before" date stamped on it. When we talk about this topic in classes, participants share the sense of urgency they feel to accomplish something, get somewhere in their careers, resolve age-old hurts and heal deep wounds. They rarely connect this sense of urgency to a fear that it will be over before they can achieve their goals. This drivenness comes through especially in those who come to the program suffering from stress-related illnesses. Like everything, what we practice in life, becomes our strongest skill when we are under stress.

What are you practicing right now? Physical injury and illness are the killing ground of our relationship with our body. This is where the feelings of betrayal and rage surface and the body becomes the battlefield between who we thought we were and who we have become. Illness and injury also point back to our mortality and the uncertainty of life. This is the most potent wakeup call we can get. In classes, we try not to be facile about the shock and resistance most people have to these events. These are not "gifts" or "welcomed guests." Hearing the diagnosis of our illness or the consequences of our injury is the voice of that no-nonsense coach who is saying, *"What can you practice right now?"*

Generosity towards ourselves is often inconceivable to most of us. We equate being generous to ourselves with being selfish. We also deflect self-generosity onto others by claiming it does us good to do good for others. While it is true that being generous to others can be a source of joy, it is more usual to hear participants talk about "doing" for others to exhaustion and resentment. That is not generosity; and when we probe deeper into the motivations for "giving to death" we hear a range of fears from needing to please to needing to control.

Because of the realities of our life (we age, die, get ill), it's important to look at what giving really means. What does it really mean to be generous to our body? What would it look like? When we ask this question in class, we get a variety of humorous answers: a million dollars so we don't have to work, a maid, a butler, a pool boy! Once the laughter subsides, we begin to look for the ways we can be generous (and not break the bank). At this point, something interesting happens: it becomes evident that we aren't used to thinking about generosity in other than large terms such as the big lottery win, the huge lifestyle transformation.

Strange to say, generosity takes careful planning and sometimes hard work. To meet ourselves with mercy and tenderness is hard because we are already hard task masters trained in a culture that does not value these virtues. Think about the comments you might get if you tell your colleagues you're taking a three-week vacation or a day at the spa. Or even an extended holiday weekend to be with your family. The comments may be well-meaning in their jest but it will likely be around the theme of whether you deserve it or that you are taking advantage of their willingness to cover for you: "Must be nice," "Wish I had time like that," or "I'd love to have your life!"

So start small. Like any work-out, we build endurance. Waking up, ask yourself, "What can I do that is generous to me?" Driving to work, eating lunch, meeting the demands of bosses, colleagues, and friends are opportunities to monitor how the scale of generosity shifts. Are we aware of the ways in which we are constantly responding to the requests of others? Do we feel open and easeful in responding or tight and reluctant? Are we aware of our resources and how we may be giving people access to them? What is being asked of our body in these requests? The late night at work, the missed lunches or suppers, the physical impact of our tasks create the conditions that wear down resilience.

Lucinda Varley and John Dalla Costa wrote a beautiful book called *Being Generous: the Art of Right Living* . They define true generosity as being regenerative. Being generous to others must replenish the wider system that gives just as giving to ourselves must replenish the well from which it is drawn. We want to be careful here to point out that we are not asking ourselves to be bean counters or to act in a *quid pro quo* manner. Instead we are asking ourselves what resources are available that make giving a gift and not a task. Sometimes it is true that we have to give when there's barely anything in the tank. However, that would not be useful, even if generous, unless we have the refill station lined up around the corner. In simple terms, we're practicing giving in a way that is sustainable and which does not deprive us over the long term of our desire and ability to be generous.

Most course participants find it easier to engage with generosity for themselves when it's small and simple: a warm bath at night, taking a walk, taking the time to shop for food they like, a glass of wine (with moderation in mind). It's also important to see the meditations like the Body Scan as times of generosity to ourselves. Thirty or forty-five minutes to really get in touch with the signals our body is sending to our brain allows us to listen deeply to what is really needed right now.

Setting physical limits by saying "Enough" is the heart and soul of practicing awareness of the body. As we attend to the signals sent from the body to our brain, we can begin to clarify the edges at which we tend to play. We can begin to discern when and how to really push the body and when to protect it from over-use. This is a difficult balance to understand, again because we live in a culture that is driven in many subtle ways. An example may be useful here.

After a prolonged period of inactivity, Lynette decided to return to jogging with some trepidation about its impact on her fibromyalgia symptoms. She enrolled in a training course and looked forward to the evening and weekend morning runs that seemed calibrated gently to completing a 5 km race in age-appropriate time. The first two or three weeks of training classes were exciting and there were surprising milestones passed. By the third and fourth week, it became apparent that her physical condition rather than the coach was going to set the pace. There began the battle of self-concepts and the expectations of others. It was really difficult to listen to the body which said, "You can run twice a week, even three, IF you pay close attention to the pace." The rest of the class surged forward running at what was a blistering pace. Each class became an exercise in mindfulness to hold the pace that would ensure getting to the end of the route with some sense of accomplishment and have something left over for work the next day.

It wasn't easy to hold steady when the pack was gradually racing out of sight. It wasn't easy realizing that pushing the pace would give a huge boost in ego in this moment but would mean pain for days after. A compassionate approach meant stepping back to see the bigger picture. It required softening to the reality of illness yet holding that strong back to sustain the practice of wellness just as it is. It was practice in the life that she had and not the one she used to have or wanted for herself at this age.

As we are learning, setting physical limits is not about hemming ourselves in or crawling into a dark hole and closing the door behind us. It's finding that edge at which we can play with what is possible.

Compassionate Speech with respect to our body is a challenge. In our clinical practice where we meet with individuals, the majority of the work is in challenging self-talk that is derogatory, diminishing, and devaluing. Patients who have experienced physical injury express deep disgust for how they believe they must now look to others. Those who have developed illnesses that manifest as tremors or fatigue refer to their bodies in terms that border on self-loathing and hatred. The language is intense and often not even what they would say to their worst enemy.

Before we can speak with kindness to ourselves, we need to see our body as a friend and not an enemy. This is hard when we've never cultivated a sense of partnership with the body. As we said earlier, the body tends to be a container for the much-valued mind and a means or a tool for getting what we want. When it fails us, it makes sense to feel let down, especially if it fails for reasons outside our control or anticipation. A compassionate approach is to see that, as in any partnership, things happen which change the form of the relationship but not the quality. Although in our case, the quality may need to change too!

We ask participants to think about their body in the same terms as someone they love who needs support. We explore all the ways in which we can "sit and have tea" with our body, chatting about things inconsequential or of deep importance. What does your body share over tea with you? What do you respond with that is supportive and caring? What is the quality of mercy you bring to your tone, your choice of words, your concept of this container of your dreams and desires?

It's important to qualify that we are not talking about "cheerleading" our body. Approaches that are not based in reality tend to fail quickly. More than that, we are not trying to motivate but to understand, to empathize with our own predicament. Due to conditions beyond our understanding, we have come to see our life as restricted by a rebellious, uncooperative entity (i.e. the body). This is what we need to change. In other words we need to change this stance that is aggressive and ultimately self-injurious. We do that by changing our patterns of speech which create and foster our perspective of ourselves.

Mindful Consumption with respect to the body supports our capacity to recover from our excesses. Or at the very least, we learn to understand our rationalizations of what has just been consumed. Entering the terms "weight loss diet" into an internet search engine garnered 28.6 million links. "Diet" generated 134 million links. "Healthy diet" showed there were 33.3 million websites ready to tell us how to attain their definition of good health. "Mindful consumption" only registered 2.24 million. That's still a lot of places where we can learn about mindful consumption. Relatively speaking, however, there's a greater perceived market for dieting than for becoming healthy through lifestyle change.

Participants in the course raise important issues of eating well. Most of us are fairly well educated in the food pyramid or have a general understanding of good foods. Probably the only sticky point tends to arise around coffee and alcohol intake. Those are more issues of endurance - "I need the caffeine to get through the day!" - and socialization - "It's hard to explain not drinking alcohol to my family & friends who drink." It's important to reflect on the factors that promote mindful eating habits rather than what is good food and what is not. Suffice to say anything in excess is not a good thing; on the other hand, all things in moderation can be boring.

When we eat, it's important to know we are eating. This sounds trite but is so very true if we are to accurately monitor our body's signals of satisfaction and satiation sent to the brain. Eating lunch at the computer while catching up on the never-ending flow of emails or grabbing a donut on the run to another "lunch-time" meeting has the effect of putting the body on alert. This diverts its systems to processing the flow of events and not to the flow of digestive juices. Take a moment to actually time how long it takes to quietly (and efficiently) eat your meal during a work day. Take the time as well to see what impedes eating dinner without the flurry of activity or the blare of sound systems. It may be a surprise to learn what is possible.

We can also focus on the food we eat and the beverages we drink as occasions to practice mindful consumption. Other aspects of mindful consumption include the environment and body in relation to its environment. Sitting hunched over the computer keyboard does not facilitate digestion nor does racing from one place to another. Similarly, slouched in an arm chair or sofa while watching TV does not promote awareness of what and how much is being consumed. These are hard-won habits we may be loathe to give up, however, allowing ourselves to experience a different softer approach may reveal fascinating insights to our way of consuming.

In an interesting but unexpected turn of events both of us required significant dental work in the same year. Wearing braces at any age is difficult but at our age, the rituals of mouth pieces that had to be put in and taken out around meals became a challenge to old habits. Initially, we met this transition as a means of developing mindful eating habits. We anticipated eating slowly and carefully, learning in the everyday to savor food and relish drinks. This is only part of what actually happened. The shocking revelation was how much of our evenings had become infused with "snacking" which we had graciously termed "grazing." With the inconvenience of having to attend to the braces and brush after each snack was consumed, "snacking" became impossible.

Suddenly, the body's addiction became apparent and there were several very uncomfortable and agitated evenings of withdrawal. As we realized what we had been cultivating, it became apparent that it was easy to call something "mindful eating" and assume that by definition it was a healthy behaviour. An open stance to the concept revealed it to be just another way of occupying the mind at the cost of the body.

In the table attached we have listed examples of behaviours we can practice to cultivate each skillful habit. Choose which skillful habit you would like to focus on for this week and which activity suits you at this time. Write it in the space below the example. You may have noticed that the five habits flow into each other. An act of generosity can be to eat mindfully which can be to cultivate respect for our physical vulnerability and so on. So, to practice one of the skillful habits is in effect to practice all of them. Nevertheless, pick one square of the chart and engage in it whole-heartedly for the week.

Continuing Your Practice

Body Scan Alternate the Body Scan with the Awareness of Breath meditation this week. Notice the breath as it moves through your body. Notice how the breath conditions the body – tight versus loose, tense versus relaxed. Meditation instructions can be found in Appendix B.

Breathing Space Sit in a quiet place and follow the breath. Notice the In breath and the Out breath: the texture, temperature, flow. Do it 6 times this week for 3 minutes each. Use the breath to steady yourself in situations, to notice when you are caught in a story, to bring yourself to "what is".

Mindful Bells Continue to practice with various stimuli in your environment to bring you back to the breath. Log it in the Record of Daily Practice.

Unpleasant Experiences Complete the table of Unpleasant Experiences (Appendix A). Notice what it is about the event that you feel is unpleasant. What do you notice about your body? What did your breathing feel like? What thoughts did you have? How are the judgmental thoughts infusing the event?

Five Skillful Habits Commit to one square in the 5 Skillful Habits grid related to the body, bringing mindfulness to the activity you have chosen.

Five Skillful Habits to Cultivate for the Body

Habit to train	Training examples
1. Respect for mortality	Exercise
2. Generosity	Rest, sleep in
3. Respect of limits	Note when fatigued, appropriate pain monitoring, say No appropriately
4. Compassionate speech	Notice something positive and say it
5. Mindful consumption	Limit snacks, take time for lunch

Record of Daily Practice – Weeks 3-6

Note each time you have practiced the Body Scan/Sitting Meditation or the "bells of mindfulness". Write your observations about each experience.

Day/Date	Body Scan	Bell of Mindfulness	Observations
Day 1 Date:	Y N	Type:	
Day 2 Date:	Y N	Type:	
Day 3 Date:	Y N	Type:	
Day 4 Date:	Y N	Type:	
Day 5 Date:	Y N	Type:	
Day 6 Date:	Y N	Type:	
Day 7 Date:	Y N	Type:	

CHAPTER 4:
Awareness of Emotions

Our intention in this chapter: Our emotional nature is the artist's palette of our experiences. It is the color and hue of what arises internally and washes over us. It is the way we develop an understanding of what is unfolding in each moment. A practice of mindfulness of the emotions begins with softening ourselves to the experience and strengthening our capacity to contain the tides of our internal life.

Awareness of Emotions

It is safe to say that we come to mindfulness hoping for a life that is peaceful and filled with joy. We have a desire for calm, an ability to just enjoy what is happening at the moment, and not being consumed by worry or physical pain. We want to reconnect, not only with the ones we love, but with our own capacity for living fully and fearlessly. Often we are tired of feeling depressed, angry, hurt, or numb. Not only do we want more of what we all believe the good parts of life contain, we want less of the bad stuff.

Sometimes there is a strong resistance to the idea that the only way to experience what is pleasant is to be willing to enter into what is unpleasant. This brings up all our misperceptions about emotions and our life as emotional beings. Similar to the relationship we have to our bodies, we have an ambivalent relationship with our emotional states. On the one hand, we tend to be very possessive about our emotional lives. It's not unusual for people to feel their emotional states are being devalued when these arising waves of sensation are defined as "physiological" events. On the other hand, we tend to separate ourselves from an image of "emotionality." It's important to know the difference, so, let's take a moment to understand what is meant by these two aspects our emotional lives.

Up- and Down-Regulating Our System

As we practice with the Body Scan and the Awareness of Breath meditations which increase awareness of the way our body speaks to us, we may begin to experience clusters of physiological sensations we label "sadness," "anxiety," "joy," "calm." Usually when we first start to practice, we might have more of the so-called negative (unpleasant) experiences than the positive (pleasant) ones. We may also neglect or dismiss neutral experiences. Lying down or sitting in meditation, we soften ourselves to these arising waves of feelings. Sometimes it can feel calming, sometimes it can feel like tidal surges that come from nowhere. It's important to know that whatever unfolds on the cushion is a reflection of what is going on in our day-to-day life. Due to lack of time to defuse these waves, we tend to absorb the force of their striking and inevitably defer processing the impact on our system.

To see how our physiology works in everyday life, let's go back to that drive to work. We got into the car already feeling a bit tender because of our "fast forwarding" through toiletries and breakfast. In other words, while showering, we were likely thinking about what or even whether we had time to have breakfast, had we done everything necessary to get the kids off to school, put all the work papers together for that meeting later today? At the kitchen table, sucking back a coffee, we're likely planning the route to work so we can get a few extra minutes to meet whatever mess is already percolating there.

On the drive, we're wondering if the other route might have been better, had our colleague put together what was promised for that 2 p.m. meeting, how are we going to wrap that up in time to get the kids... oh and dinner... when there's a blare of car horns, shaking fists, and other non-verbal signals of displeasure from the car that has just cut us off. Our heart is beating wildly now, we're feeling shaky, and our palms may become sweaty. We react with our own sign language. We're offended, angry, enraged, feeling attacked, misunderstood and looking for revenge. Somehow we get to work. By then we've constructed a story which protects us from judgment and justifies our response.

Two things occurred in this timeline scenario. First, our physiology was ramping up slowly through the morning and then went into overdrive. Second, we reacted with behaviours that have certain socially-constructed labels and which draw on previous experiences. Shaking = anxiety, shock, surprise; "sign language" = anger, aggressive confrontation. The two are intricately interconnected. Given the event, it is consistent to label the physiological reactions as anxiety, shock, aggression, and anger. These are responses to a feeling of threat. However, under other more benign circumstances (at the top of a ski hill), the physiological sensations of heart beating faster, feeling shaky, and sweaty palms may have been interpreted differently (excitement, nervousness, etc.).

> Remember the exercise of noticing unpleasant experiences?
>
> What did you notice happening in your body during the events? How long did the sensations last after the event was over?

In other words, what we label our internal experience depends on the external context and our prior experience in such situations. Depending on our previous experience with aggression or feeling unable to protect ourselves, the incident may have us generating stories about vulnerability, victimhood, helplessness, or self/other blame. If our history includes denial of our emotional state or interpretation of emotions as showing weakness, we may engage in pushing those emotions away. Once we get to work, our story of the crazy driver may exclude our reactions or we may reframe the reactivity to be something the other person deserved.

Avoiding Our Emotional Experience

This brings us to the second stance to our emotional lives: *emotional avoidance*. Some of us prefer to live separate lives from our emotional nature. We may believe we are better off taking a very analytical view of the world so that our decisions and actions are based on "facts." What we hope by leaning on this strategy is that our actions are "defensible" because no one can accuse us of having acted irrationally. In fact, all decisions we make are based on our preferences, our judgment of our actions, and our assess-ment of threat or safety. In other words, our choices are grounded in our emotional nature. Likes and dislikes guide our preferences. Comfort or concern with certain actions guides our morals, ethics, and motivation. Risk assessments activate or inhibit behaviours that will ensure survival. We don't tend to think of these influences as part of our emotional nature; however, just because we are composed in our decision-making does not mean that we were emotionless when we made it.

We may also distrust the seemingly irrational side of ourselves and feel it is best pushed away each time it surfaces. Emotions appear to surge and recede unpredictably and often inconveniently. Laughter or anger erupt at inappropriate times, tears are triggered by innocuous events (like TV commercials), or sometimes everything goes cold and inaccessible just when an expression of warmth or support is crucial! At no time in our lives do we feel more out of control than this and at no time is it more crucial to open ourselves to the very existence of these feelings without adding shame or blame to the mix.

Emotional Regulation System

Kate was a determined practitioner with a good understanding of what would be required to meet this challenge. She began the program with the intention to be open to whatever her body and mind presented to her. The initial meditation practices and the discipline were a struggle for Kate as she practiced staying with the emotions that arose. Initially she only managed a moment or two before reactively switching tracks. Then she began to take a stance of attentive listening to the emotions. Instead of labeling the waves of feelings as awful, terrible or fearful, she noticed if it was pleasant, neutral, or unpleasant. She watched the stories and hopped on and off trains that took her away from the experience. Slowly, Kate began to notice that emotions had a beginning, a progress through her awareness, followed by dissipation. Knowing this, she was able to stay with the process with composure.

Dolores struggled with the agitation that arose every time she sat still. In her history, being still was a sure sign of becoming a target for a violent parent. Her whole body was constantly prepped for evasive action; her physiology was ramped to high alert, a steady state of preparedness that required large infusions of caffeine to sustain. She was so well-trained in using this fired-up state that she thrived on the adrenaline rush of her job and constant calls to rescue somebody. However, when her day ended, Dolores was consumed by the fear of the stillness. To counteract the feelings of agitation, she worked out, ate ferociously, and leaned towards high action, intense movies or games. In her drive to escape the fear that surfaced when she was not occupied with some passion or the other, Dolores had developed an addictive approach to dealing with her emotions.

Current research on the brain is clarifying how our emotional system works and how mindfulness can modify some of the tangled wiring we cultivate given the life we lead. Paul Gilbert, author of *Compassion-Focused Therapy*, describes three systems that regulate our emotional states: a threat-protection system, a reward seeking system, and a soothing system. Our genetic and learning history shapes and trains these systems. For example, Kate's anxiety-based responses would arise in the threat-protection system; Dolores' actions would be driven from the threat-protection system as well, however her reward system (enjoyment from the adrenaline rush) would also be in overdrive trying to keep the emotional state regulated. Mindfulness practices allow for a space between their perception of threat and their typical reactivity. In that space, through the Five Skillful Habits, they learned to activate their soothing system and make different choices.

Under stress, the thinking process alone is enough to arouse our physiology and set off our alarm bells. Past history of what threats we encountered and their impact on us plays a powerful role in creating and storing emotional memories. When current situations evoke these emotional memories that are deeply embedded in our system, beliefs of our vulnerability are also triggered. If we can soothe ourselves, we have a chance to step back and see the situation as something happening now. Effectively, we can get ahead of the feeling that it is going to have the same outcome as our previous experiences. For example, the argument with our boss has different possibilities of resolution if we can see it as happening here and now rather than a *fait accompli* based on our story of "always losing battles."

Let's look at three ways we reinforce unhealthy reactivity to situations and three ways to soothe our emotional system.

Feeding the Fear, Clouding the Vision

In the face of a perceived or real threat to our survival, we react in one of three ways: push away what we don't want, cling to what we want, or feel frozen because we don't understand what's happening. In Buddhist terms, these are called the three poisons; passion, aggression, and confusion. (The older terms were anger, greed, and ignorance, respectively.) They are toxic because they cloud our judgment in the assessment of external danger signals in a situation. In short, we react in controlling ways to these threatening external events hoping our strategies will make us feel safer. In fact, they actually only make our inner emotional state more intense.

Internally, as we experience our emotional state intensifying, maybe even becoming intolerable by triggered memories or negative thought patterns, sadness, anger, and confusion cycle around spiraling out of control. Our need to control the cascade of emotions is expressed through the three stances of passion, aggression, and confusion. If we feel our deprivation can be soothed by acquiring an object or praise from someone, we become demanding, holding onto the idea or behaviour sometimes past the point of its usefulness. When we feel thwarted or disregarded in some way, we respond with rejection of what is happening. When we lack sufficient information or fail to understand what is actually happening to us, we feel confused, indecisive, and unable to move one way or the other. We lose perspective and begin to see ourselves as weak or irrational.

> *Read the poem "The Guesthouse" by Rumi. Who are these visitors? How do you greet them? Can you really keep them out of your guesthouse?*

The Guesthouse[4]

This being human is a guest-house.
Every morning a new arrival.

A joy, a depression, a meanness,
some momentary awareness comes
as an unexpected visitor.

Welcome and entertain them all!
Even if they're a crowd of sorrows,
who violently sweep your house
empty of its furniture,
still, treat each guest honorably.
He may be clearing you
out for some new delight.

The dark thought, the shame, the malice,
meet them at the door laughing,
and invite them in.

Be grateful for whoever comes,
because each has been sent
as a guide from beyond.

Both Kate and Dolores had to work hard to let go of their self-protective habits. These behaviours had served them well in the past but were now obstacles undermining their desires to live differently. In Kate's case, her anxiety attacks kept her from advancing both in work and in relationships. Events triggered demanding behaviours such as asking for reassurance consequently leaving her feeling lost or abandoned when it wasn't available to her. Dolores on the other hand was beginning to feel the exhaustion of always being on high alert which meant she was unable to develop trusting relationships with herself or others. Aggression followed closely

---

4   *The Essential Rumi*, Translated by Coleman Barks with John Moyne, A.J. Arberry & Reynold Nicholson, Castle Books, Copyright© 1995. Reprinted by kind permission of Mr. Coleman Barks.

on irritation with others or energy would be used up clinging or trying to push for her way of dealing with problems at work or at home.

Attention, Breath, Calm

As we can see much of our emotional life is lived below the level of awareness. Responses are affected by our genes as well as our learning history and are often set in motion well before we can know something is brewing. In most cases, we are only aware of the depth of our feelings about something when the behaviours are activated. In order to develop more skillful and beneficial responses, it is necessary to pay attention to the early warning signals of unpleasant sensations which may transform into emotionally reactive behaviours. Thankfully, it's as simple as A-B-C.

A: Paying attention means systematically returning to the activity of the moment regardless of the stories that say the mental "problem solving" is more important. As we're showering, we pay attention to showering. If a thought or emotional sensation arises, we note this ("worry," "planning," etc.) and come back to attending to the activity of the moment. This has two effects. First, it strengthens the association between brain and behaviour, allowing the brain to "log" exactly what an action feels like (pleasant, unpleasant, neutral). This cultivates clarity of and trust in our own experiences. Second, it short-circuits the wiring that supports spiraling out from worry to anxiety, sadness to depression, and so on.

B: : The breath is a barometer of our physical and emotional state. Paying attention to the length and quality of our breathing, we begin to learn how to read our physical and emotional states more accurately. Long, slow breaths may elicit steadiness

> *The Goblet: a 3-minute breathing exercise*
>
> *First minute: open your awareness to your experience. Imagine it's a bowl in which everything is held without attraction or aversion. Visualize it as the bowl of the goblet.*
>
> *Second minute: bring your attention to your breathing at your nostrils or abdomen. Feel the sensation of the breath. Visualize this narrowing as the stem of the goblet.*
>
> *Third minute: ground yourself in the body. Feel the floor under your feet if standing or solidity of your seat if sitting. Visualize this is the wide base of the goblet.*
>
> *For a detailed script see Appendix D*

or calm. Short, ragged breaths may be associated with tension, anger, or fear. As we attune ourselves to the length and quality of our breathing we develop a lexicon of our internal state. Then, without manipulating the breath, we can begin to experiment with our breathing rhythm to see how it affects our emotional system. We experience the interconnectedness of breath and our inner experience. Now, when our mind has wandered into sticky places that evoke unsteadiness, we can use the breath as a way station to return to our activity of the moment. Paying attention to the breath disengages the worrying, wandering mind and steadying the breath settles it.

C: Combining our practice of returning to the moment's activity through steadied breathing results in a calming effect. This is the soothing third system Gilbert talks about. When we can self-soothe through mindfulness practices, we teach ourselves not to be fearful of our emotional repertoire. We can begin to experience the range of human emotion from agitation to calm, anger to compassion without pushing away the unpleasant or clinging to the pleasant.

By softening and opening to the full range of our emotional life, we transform our rigid, judgmental assessment that expressing emotions is a weakness or a sign of irrationality. The three toxins of passion, aggression, and confusion can shift, with practice, towards generosity, clarity, and fearlessness. Not only do we develop clarity about our unpleasant experiences, we can also become generous in giving ourselves the full experience of pleasant events. When we can't predict how something will impact on us, when we are not in control, opening to this experience cultivates fearlessness in the face of not knowing.

Cultivating Compassionate Awareness of Our Emotions through the Five Skillful Habits

We'd like to make a really important point here as we dive into the practices. Our emotions are not neatly packaged units that we stack up on a closet shelf. We do wish it were that way. There is deep wisdom in the air steward's advice when a plane is landing: "Please be careful opening the overhead bins as the contents may have shifted in transit." Our tolerance for the range and intensity of our emotions changes as we transition from closed to open, mind-distant to heart-felt. So, please be gentle in your practice. Attend to what is arising and how it is arising in the meditations, and to your capacity to be present with it. While it is often said that in meditation we do not take prisoners, it is probably more useful and beneficial to just not create the battlefield.

Respecting our mortality is not easy to conceptualize in the context of our emotional life. It may feel more relevant if we think of our body as having physical limitations as a result of its inherently delicate coping system. The central nervous system manages the impact of the world and its demands through a finely tuned process of chemical communication. When it is stressed, as all systems are in the process of living, it responds in a measured way to activate and then shut down our response mechanisms.

Take a moment and think about the connection between feeling anger and the internal organs that are affected. We know that when the body is required to respond to a demand, the mechanisms of coping involve the central nervous system and release of chemicals to activate muscles, heart rate, and breathing. The endpoint of this response cycle is the release of cortisol to regulate the amygdala and hippocampus which play an important role in perceiving sensations and putting the experience into context and memory.

The amygdala notes the presence of sensations in the body that signal the need for fight-or-flight (we'll discuss this more in a later chapter). It does not have the capacity to understand or rationalize the event; it just records the flow of the experience. The hippocampus logs the conditions of the event and plays a role in making sense out of the event. It takes sensations of heart beating fast, sweating, feeling nauseous and puts it into a context of an event like a close call on the highway. This way we have a connection between what we feel and what we know is going on. We can put words to the feeling: "I was so angry when that truck almost ran me off the road!"

When stress is chronic or very intense, this system is overloaded and the hippocampus is damaged. The ability to hold and place things in memory and to make sense of our experience is reduced or, in extreme cases, lost. This means we perceive sensations arising but have trouble making sense of it. Our emotional world becomes chaotic and our internal responses can be confusing. Physically, our body is unable to determine when to respond and when to turn off the response system. As the nervous system is challenged to a greater and greater degree, we begin to develop a vulnerability to stress-related disorders.

Recognizing and accepting our internal vulnerability is the first step to taking care of ourselves. Identifying the emotional states accurately is a challenge in itself however the advantage is in knowing exactly what is happening. It also allows us to resolve the emotional state at an earlier stage when it is not as much of a challenge to calm ourselves.

Generosity to our emotional life is a challenge for us especially if we view emotions as a weakness. We are very welcoming of pleasant emotions but tend to block unpleasant ones. Often we treat them like unwelcomed guests by ignoring them, shutting them out or reacting to them with shame and disappointment. When we read Rumi's poem, we may feel incredulous about letting in "the dark thought, the shame, the malice." It might seem unthinkable to encourage meeting guilt, anger, or cynicism so that we can better hear what they're trying to tell us. Perhaps it can help to imagine that strong emotions like anger may be representatives of unacknowledged, buried emotions. We may react with anger because our feelings of powerlessness or being disregarded are not allowed to surface. We may express meanness, disinterest, or coldness because we have learned to hide our vulnerability and need for others.

Taking an open stance to these unpleasant emotions gives us an opportunity to see them clearly and to see what the deeper feelings are. Be present when angry or sad. Identify the sensations that go along with the emotional label to see how you are defining a particular emotion. Sometimes we call something sad when it's actually something else. We may label our reaction as "weak" when it may be "frustrated." Learning the connection between the sensation and what we've trained ourselves to call it allows us to correct our self-perception. As we discussed in the second chapter, by the time the emotion is felt, it is already too late to avoid it. By welcoming it, as difficult as that might be, we spare ourselves the added suffering of invalidating our experience.

Setting emotional limits is critical when we are in relationships that are rife with intense emotional tones. Whatever our capacity to be empathetic, we are receptive to the emotions of others. We feel happy when we are with happy people, sad when with sad people. We resonate and respond to the feeling tones of those around us. Sometimes this can be to the extent that even if we are happy, sad people can bring us down. In helping family or friends, we might find ourselves in situations where we are giving of our time and resources freely yet feeling dragged down by the interactions. Or, at work, we may be in a toxic environment or relationship that saps our energy. We may tend to stay too long in an angry conversation hoping for a better outcome. We may tolerate a friend's neediness when we are low on our own resources.

It is important to monitor the impact of our interactions on our emotional state. This is especially important when we are in a position of care giving or play a supportive role in work or family. It allows us to monitor more accurately what resources we have to give and to spare for ourselves. It prevents others from making assumptions about our capacity to carry them and encourages them to develop their own capacity to care for themselves.

Compassionate speech towards ourselves when we experience intense emotions is the groundwork of self-care. If we've grown up with messages that expressing or even feeling emotions is a reflection of being damaged, we may have internalized the denigrating, dismissing language of our childhood. Many men speak of being told they were weak when they cried or that their anger was so destructive that no one would survive. They may even have observed and interpreted their fathers' or role models' behaviours that way. Women tend to talk of having their sadness or anger dismissed; often told to "get over it" they feel there is no room for them to express a normal response to painful events.

It's no surprise then that we have a hard time speaking to ourselves in ways that are kind and tolerant of our emotional experiences. Our speech is judgmental and harsh; we are often doing internally exactly what we wish others would not do externally. To work at turning this reactive mode around takes dedicated practice.

Write down phrases and words you can use that allow yourself to be present to an emotion without judging it. Listen to the type of language and quality of the tone you use to speak to yourself. Is it encouraging, comforting, supportive? This doesn't mean giving yourself license to indulge in an emotional state. It does mean allowing yourself the space to observe what is arising and whether you are adding to the initial discomfort. Ask yourself, "What might happen if I let go of trying to get a solution?" Write down all the answers that surface. Now ask, "What am I really holding onto?"

Mindful consumption is the flip side of respecting your limits in emotional situations. The behaviours and their impact are subtle. We may be out with friends and find ourselves engaging in negative discussions about others. We may seek support and end up angrier because the other person had fed our frustration. We may decide to watch a movie or listen to songs that reflect our sadness or anger hoping for validation but feeling worse at the end of it.

It is possible to include emotionally driven eating here as well. The agitation we feel when we're ramped up from a difficult day or interchange with others may feel like it needs internal comforting. If we have a habit of self-soothing through food, it's important to observe the sensations carefully. The management of emotionally driven eating is outside the scope of this guidebook; however, we have included a number of great books in the Reference section for your use. Please practice fiercely on this particular issue because it is so closely tied to the first skillful habit, our mortality.

Observe carefully as well, the impact of TV shows, movies, websites, and books on your state of mind. That's not to say we shouldn't enjoy what these media offer us. The key of practice is entering into them with a clear intention and in remaining attentive to the impact of these activities if we inadvertently get caught in them. If you are seeking relaxation, then consider your choice of media and its content. If you are seeking validation of your feelings, then consider if the choice will give the appropriate validation or just allow you to stay stuck in the story about the feelings. Misery loves company – but only the company that allows us to stay stuck to it. In fact, Misery is a jealous guardian of getting on with our lives and will resist anything that leads us out of our tangled thoughts.

In the table attached, we have listed examples of behaviours we can practice to cultivate each skillful habit. Choose which skillful habit you would like to focus on for this week and which activity suits you at this time. Write your chosen activity in the space provided below the example. You may have noticed that the five habits flow into each other. An act of generosity can be to eat mindfully which can be to cultivate respect for our physical vulnerability and so on. Remember, to practice one of the skillful habits is, in effect, to practice all of them.

Continuing Your Practice

Awareness of Breath Meditation Practice the meditation every day this week. Pay close attention to the arising of sensations you label as types of emotion. Notice the arising, duration and dissolution of the emotion. Log your efforts in the Record of Daily Practice provided in Chapter 3.

Breathing Space Meditation Practice the 3-minute breathing meditation as often as you can this week. Use the breath to steady yourself in situations, especially when emotions arise or there is any anticipation of emotional reactivity.

Mindful Bells Continue to practice with various stimuli in your environment to bring you back to the breath. Log it in the Record of Daily Practice.

Five Skillful Habits Select a habit to cultivate this week. Make note of the rising and falling of emotional states during your practice.

Day of Mindfulness This is a good time to schedule a day during which you can practice your mindfulness skills. The instructions for a Do-It-Yourself day are in Appendix E. It is best, however, if you can find a place to practice with others. Check out the local practice centers to see what they offer. We also recommend a regular DIY day to sustain your practice.

Five Skullful Habits to Cultivate for Emotions

Habit to train	Training examples
1. Respect for mortality	Note how negative emotions lead to physical problems such as hypertension
2. Generosity	Allow yourself to acknowledge the presence of guilt, anger, happiness, etc.
3. Respect of limits	Note negative emotions and sit with them as long as is comfortable for you
4. Compassionate speech	Try to approach all emotions with an attitude of curiosity
5. Mindful Consumption	Note the emotional effects of what we are watching on television, emotional eating

CHAPTER 5:
Awareness of Sensations

Our intention in this chapter: *The messengers that carry information to our brain are sensations that arise from contact between our body and our environment. They carry the raw data that informs the brain and allows it to activate our response. The final message is a complex integration of past experience, current meaning, and coping skills. Mindfulness practices allow us to step back from the past storylines that can derail this process, to see them as guides and not inevitable truths, thereby allowing the body and mind to collaborate as partners.*

Awareness of Sensations

The practice of mindfulness is an *embodied* practice. That means it arises from an awareness of our body as it communicates with our mind which in turn activates the body to respond. To embody mindfulness practice is to be aware of this interchange between body and mind as both participant and gentle observer. This cycle of communication relies on reading the basic information units in the body: the sensations we feel. Through our practice, we have slowly peeled away the conceptual aspects of our experience. By slowing down and observing the story-telling assumptions about our strengths and weaknesses, projections from the past and into the future become the focus of our work. In the previous chapter, we connected with our emotions as sensations we feel and not as concepts or labels. Now we will explore these sensations in the broader landscape of our experience.

Sensations can occur externally at the interface between body and the object of contact or internally as an expression of ease, discomfort, or pain.

The feeling of touching a flower and feeling our heartbeat are examples of an external and internal sensation, respectively. As rich as our experience may be, we tend to have a limited lexicon when it comes to naming sensations. When we go to a physician who examines our pain, it's not unusual to draw a blank when we are asked what that pain feels like. In therapy sessions, our patients tend to have the same trouble when asked to describe a sensation they notice when they speak of an emotional experience. One explanation is that we tend to lump together labels signifying emotion with those that underlie the emotion. Another explanation is that we become so quickly caught up in trying to resolve the sensation (especially unpleasant ones) that we don't hang around trying to find a label for it.

Because the most prominent and vivid experience of sensations is usually found when we are in physical pain, we will focus much of the exploration through the lens of physical and physiological sensations. However, emotional pain, as we learned in the last chapter, also appears through powerful sensations; these are difficult to name and we will have to practice more diligently.

Ashley's back pain was often overwhelming. It started as a sharp, sudden jab in her lower back and then became an ache that sometimes burned along her leg. When she came for the intake session, she had trouble describing the sensations. It was all just PAIN and it was EVERYWHERE. She would become tearful and explained how she felt like a failure. She thought that people believed she was faking because she simply had no words for the sensations.

Jason's pain was different. He described it as feeling like he had the flu but without the obvious symptoms. Dull, aching, weary, tingling, throbbing were some terms he had learned over time to convey his experience. Yet to Jason these were too discrete because the overall feeling was one of a foggy disconnect with his environment and any interpersonal exchange. Jason felt anxious that he came across as disinterested or bored when, in fact, he felt intense fatigue as he tried to get through "molasses moments."

From a wide base of research into both physical and emotional pain, we have begun to understand how the brain uses sensations to inform and activate responses. Information flows in through the physical portals of our senses (eyes, nose, mouth, ears, and skin) and the brain is constantly washed by this stream of information. It's quite amazing that we can actually orient to what is needed in any moment (whether or not we are actually aware of doing so) and how we do that is not completely known. It's enough for our purposes here to accept that we do have some type of filter that keeps us from becoming overwhelmed with the deluge of electrical impulses speeding from the point of contact to the brain.

Not to over-simplify the process, it goes something like this:

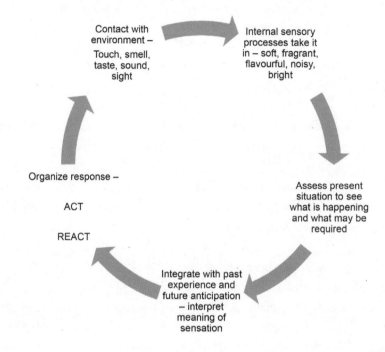

Maybe that was not such an over-simplification! Because we have this huge database of sensory information, we can quickly organize and define our experience as something familiar or novel. This is also likely why we don't become overwhelmed and is one of those times where auto-pilot is actually useful. Researchers and therapists who work with the sensorimotor dimensions of our experience describe a type of toggling between the more biologically-based processes that we don't have conscious access to and the ones with which we engage with intention. Learning the dance between this bottom-up and top-down processing is an important aspect of mindfulness practice.

As an example, Frank loves long distance drives. So, many of our vacations have been adventures to interesting places that require at least a day or two of driving to get there. As we got older, the drives required more self-care; 16 hours of driving were no longer an option. Frank also began to have knee problems which threatened to restrict the range of our drives. Not to be defeated by age and deteriorating tendons, he would push through the pain or ignore it all together. It wasn't long before our drives became long periods of tense silences as he powered through the miles. Of course, once we got to our destination, he needed a few days of recovery before he could enjoy the vacation at all.

Thankfully, Frank began his mindfulness practice about the same time the knee issue was becoming an obstacle to enjoying our vacations. He practiced letting go of the stories (the conceptual, top-down process) about his knee and aging body. He learned to use the initial sensations in the area of his knee as a reminder that he actually had a knee (bottom-up processing). Strange to say but we often forget we have body parts until the sensations are so intense that we have no choice but to attend. For Frank the early sensations were a signal that he should begin to plan a stop. As he learned not to react to the sensations, the planning not only gave him the required rest, we started finding interesting places to explore as part of the journey.

When we began our practice, we set our intention to notice the storylines that often high-jacked our experiences. We practiced through the Body Scan and the meditations to let go of the story and come into the experience itself. This was not because the stories were bad or wrong; letting go of the stories is intended to shift the filters that block our view of the whole picture. Our past experience creates a shorthand version or, in computer terms, a macro, that quickly summarizes the physical, emotional and sensorimotor sensation so that we can efficiently make a decision about an event. Most of the time, we can get away with the shorthand but it is at the cost of full awareness of what is happening. And unfortunately when we are in pain it limits the range of information that we can access.

Ashley's shorthand about her back pain was that a tingle in her leg or a twinge in her lower back was a signal that there would be weeks of excruciating pain and maybe even days lying on the hard surface of the floor. Knowing the impact of days of lost work time and the burden it placed on her family, Ashley would feel anxious and guilty. Her very protective brain eventually jumped from "twinge" to "anxiety." This was a shortcut that was neither efficient nor beneficial because it didn't take into account what was really happening at the moment.

How Is It Now?

Barry Briggs, a Zen teacher we respect very much, is fond of asking, "How is it now?" It's a lovely simple question that brings us immediately into this moment's experience. "What are you noticing?" is another great question. In cultivating the art of mindfulness, participants really struggle with the idea of coming into the sensory levels of knowing. Often they feel the meaning of their pain would be taken away and that meaning is so important because somehow it seems to justify their experience.

The paradigm shift in bringing awareness to the sensations and not the story is that we fully own our pain without need to justify it to anyone, most especially to ourselves. In other words, the pain does not have to be layered with the pages generated by the story-telling machine. In fact, when pain is layered with stories about past and future, it becomes a complicated mass of suffering. Starting with its true nature, a sensation can be a turning point for many of us who experience pain that is hard to describe (especially when there is no external evidence of injury) because staying in the realm of sensations relieves us from the burden of justifying the feeling. It just is.

In order to practice this bottom-up approach, we begin by asking what might happen if we let go of wanting the pain to end. In other words, we peel back that layer of assumptions and interpretation. As long as we are driven to get past the pain, we miss critical signals about the true nature of the pain. That in turn leads to impulsive or inappropriate decisions about managing the experience. Restraining our need to get to the end of the unpleasant experience means we have a broader database from which to assess and understand what we need. Meditation used as formal practice (30 minutes each day on the cushion or chair) is a means of strengthening our ability to stay with the sensation and not get dragged off by a persistently wandering mind.

As we practice, we cultivate our capacity to attend to the sensations without being swept away by them. This is where developing a lexicon of sensation names is important (dull, twitch, tense, quivery, pinching, pulsing, sweaty, etc.). In meditation practice, we name the experience: wandering mind, planning, anger, joy, tingling, warm, cool, and so on. We suspend the conceptual mind and come back over and over again to the experience of contact between the body and the environment. This doesn't mean we grit our teeth and hang in when things are excruciating; staying with the experience of pain means we bring an attentive awareness to just what is unfolding so that we can make an informed decision about rest, medication, and setting limits.

Jason came to class and shared his experience of a week spent shifting from his mind's need to take charge and his body's signals of the pain. He noticed that when he went with the interpretations about progress and relapse, the pain escalated because it was compounded by physical tension from self-judgements and about outcomes. When he jumped from the initial sensation, to trying to fix or prevent its presumed course, he over- or under-compensated his interventions. When he stayed with just what was happening in each moment, he was able to assess the intensity (strong, tolerable, mild) more accurately. He noticed the pain had an ebb and flow which he could attend to by using the breath. He described watching for moments when he could choose a different approach to being with it. Sometimes it meant lying down and sometimes it meant doing a bit of mindful movements (see Appendix C). It was a revelation, he said, that he didn't feel diminished by letting go of the story or by pushing away the unpleasant physical and emotional feelings.

Ashley and Jason also had to confront their need to meet everyone's expectation that they move on, get on with their lives, and stop re-playing every moment that might or might not have caused a relapse. They worried about what their bosses might say if they reported having a neutral or good day. They felt their friends might expect more if they showed up at activities that they previously avoided or could not attend. Ironically, feeling less pain or even managing the pain more skillfully is a double-edged sword. As they practiced, however, they came to see that the benefits of honouring their body's way of communicating with them far out-weighed any reaction from family or work or friends.

Cultivating Compassionate Awareness of Our Sensations through the Five Skillful Habits

In the previous chapter, we invited you to please be gentle in your practice. That invitation to compassionate awareness is also important when practicing awareness of sensations. In our culture we are over-trained to view tolerance for pain as the pinnacle of strength and fortitude. We are bombarded with images of super-athletes who drive through intense pain to achieve their goals. Or we are faced with stories of survivors of horrific world events despite physical and emotional trauma. It's hard to feel compassionate about our pain in the face of such experiences. And there's no easy answer to bridging that gap between ourselves and the athlete or survivor. All we can do is practice and allow that practice to become part of a world-wide group of people who are willing to face what is in front of them and not look away.

Cultivating awareness of our sensations using the Five Skillful Habits is very similar to our previous practice with the emotions. Bring attention to the sensations without engaging immediately in the rationalizing, questioning, or planning to fix or manage them.

Respecting our mortality by attending to sensations can mean bringing awareness to the way our bodies are communicating calm or distress. We don't like to think about it but our bodies have a limited time frame. Attending to the effects of over-indulging in food, drink, and even play alerts us when we are at the edge of well-being. Pain is the language the body uses to signal that the wear and tear is not balanced with repair. When we don't respect this micro-mortality, physical breakdown occurs.

Other areas worthy of attention are in the way we acknowledge that the body needs support. Awareness of sensations of pain or discomfort and using appropriate interventions such as medication, exercise, and diet fosters a respect for where the body is at this point in life.

Generosity towards our sensory experiences is similar to our emotional experience. Allowing the sensation to be there without pushing it away or manipulating it is an act of graciousness. Creating spaciousness around the experience and not tightening up to control it also removes the layering of more pain onto us.

Setting limits is crucial. Know when to use medication and when to rest. As we said earlier, super-athletes take one approach to dealing with pain that comes from years of hard training. Take that approach to your practice too; train to be dedicated and diligent about setting limits. By conserving energy and allowing the body to build its resilience, we can get to be super-athletes of a new kind. The sport is living an attentive life that is authentic and full.

Compassionate speech cuts away the weights that drag us down when we are in pain or struggling. When we speak harshly to ourselves about our abilities to do things or tolerate things, we drain ourselves of the energy needed to do what we need to do. Although we've cautioned against re-framing our experience too quickly, it is important to practice a realistic and accurate perspective to our feelings and efforts.

Running up against the reality that we can now do some things but not others, achieve some goals but not the ones we thought we would, can be discouraging. Speaking of these shifts in our life as failures or taking them as representation of our character undermines us. It cuts away the supports that we need to shape new habits.

Mindful consumption is perhaps the most important of the Five Skillful Habits with regard to sensations. Too often we fall into a spiral of pain and suffering, a process of consuming our experience which does not lead to well-being. Instead, notice when the mind tips over into self-indulgence from bare awareness. At what point does gentle curiosity about the edge of a sensation become a contest to see how long we can stay at that edge or a spiral into encouraging the concepts that circle around the sensation.

As before, in the table attached, we have listed examples of behaviours that cultivate each skillful habit. Choose which skillful habit you would like to focus on for this week and which activity suits you at this time. Write your chosen activity in the space provided below the example. Be realistic about what you can practice at this time. Practicing pain tolerance is not the point; however, practicing awareness of that edge between tolerable pain and the need for assistance can be a practice of curiosity and openness to experience.

Continuing Your Practice

Awareness of Breath Meditation Practice the meditation every day this week. Pay close attention to the arising of sensations and practice naming them as succinctly as you can. Notice the arising, duration and dissolution of the sensation. Use the Record of Daily Practice in Chapter 3.

Breathing Space Meditation Practice as often as you can this week. Use the breath as a means of approaching the sensations and a refuge to step back from the sensations.

Mindful Bells Continue to practice with various stimuli in your environment to bring you back to the breath.

Five Skillful Habits Select a habit to cultivate this week. Choose a habit that you feel encourages you to be compassionate with yourself. In the template, create a list of sensation words that you are particularly familiar with. Practice observing how they change.

Five Skillful Habits to Cultivate for Sensations

Habit to train	Training examples
1. Respect for mortality	Note sensations that signal health issues
2. Generosity	Allow yourself to feel the sensation without judging the experience
3. Respect of limits	Note edge of the sensation: if it is localized in the body, where does it begin on the body, where does it fade away. Discern between tolerating a sensation and gently observing it.
4. Compassionate speech	Try to approach the experience with kindness
5. Mindful Consumption	Note the effects of indulging in the sensation

CHAPTER 6:
Awareness of Thoughts

Our intention in this chapter: We live in a rapidly flowing stream of thoughts. They flow incessantly and tend to sweep us away. Whether we are aware of being carried along by a thought or not we are, and this is the root of some of our suffering. Mindfulness of our thoughts and thinking patterns help to break the autopilot forms of thinking that can lead us into negative spirals of depression or anxiety.

Awareness of Thoughts

Thoughts are our way of organizing our experience. They help us categorize, plan, problem-solve, and adapt to situations. Western philosophy and culture has come to value the rational thinking process over the so-called irrational or emotional process. Research, however, shows that the emotional system plays a very significant role in decision-making and perceiving accurately what is unfolding in the moment. We dealt with the emotion platform two chapters back and we will return to it at the end of this chapter to integrate it into the thought platform of mindfulness practices.

For now, let's attend to this process of rational decision-making and see how it can help and hinder us in our life. Hamlet's words capture the essence of our work with thoughts.

> *"There is nothing either good or bad, but thinking makes it so."*
> *- William Shakespeare, Hamlet, 2.2*

And Marcus Aurelius shows us the impact of thoughts on our spirit.

The soul becomes dyed with the color of its thoughts.

In other words, how we interpret our experience plays an important role in how we experience our life. And, that interpretation process is guided by our habitual patterns of thinking. Psychological theories explain this as an appraisal system that assesses the level of threat of an event. We respond to the experience with an intensity that we believe is necessary to ward off the perceived danger. Notice the way this is being explained: there is nothing in the explanation about absolute truth or fact.

The explanation implies that we are always assessing the correlation between our perception of threat and the fact of threat. Of course, if the perceived threat is an eighteen-wheel truck coming at you, there is no question about the absolute correlation between your perception and fact.

However, most of our experiences don't fall neatly into an absolute correlation between perception and fact. One of the reasons for that is the way we have evolved socially. The appraisal system is intended to help us survive in a very literal way. Our ancestors needed a highly sensitive system that helped differentiate between a snake and a stick, a saber-tooth tiger and a rock formation. We're wired to assess, activate, and actualize in a way that keeps us safe physically.

As social systems grew and we became interconnected in ways other than protection at a physical level, our brains developed more complex systems of appraisal and we needed to differentiate among more subtle levels of threat. The problem however is the appraisal system remained the same – more efficient, but fundamentally it is still a process of activating and deactivating the response to threat.

The Central Response System

Let's take a look at our response system before we dig into the appraisal systems and their impact on our well-being. Our physiology is made up of the Central Nervous system which includes the Brain and Spinal Cord. All of us are aware of how important the CNS is in keeping us alive and functioning. We may be less aware of the Peripheral Nervous System which is made up of the Sympathetic Nervous System (SNS) and the

Parasympathetic Nervous System (PNS).

The SNS and the PNS work to balance each other. Together, they control many of the adaptive functions needed to get us through our day. The Sympathetic NS activates the physiology so that it can meet the demands that arise throughout the day. When we wake up, our heart rate and blood pressure have to rise so that we can get on with the tasks of the day. Rising out of bed, walking to the bathroom, making decisions about meals, driving to work, taking the bus, meeting with our boss or teams, all require differing levels of activation. The Parasympathetic NS deactivates our physiology or, to put it another way, it lowers the rising heart rate and blood pressure, breathing, temperature, etc. so the system doesn't keep ramping up. There's another system called the Vagal System which acts like a cap on the overall process so we don't run amok. Under extreme and chronic stress, the vagal system is the one that gets damaged and we have trouble modulating our reactions.

Laurie Leitch and Elaine Miller-Karas who developed the Trauma Resource Model explain that the SNS and PNS also function in a range called the Resilient Zone. This range defines the upper and lower limits of our ability to adapt to the demands made of our physical and emotional system. The overall system looks like the figure below.

Nervous System

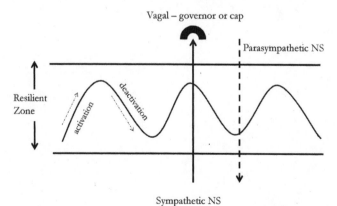

Diagram adapted from Trauma Resource Model courtesy Laurie Leitch & Elaine Miller-Karas

For most of us, the activation and deactivation will occur with little awareness as we go through our day. (Actually, by now, we hope not because we've been diligently practicing awareness of our sensations!) We get out of bed and our systems activate; we settle into breakfast or a good cup of coffee or tea and we deactivate. We get on the highway or the bus, we activate. Pull into our parking spot, we deactivate. It's not quite that absolute because there is a constant ebb and flow in meeting the events of the day and if we aren't quite practicing our breathing and mindful bells exercises, we may not be re-setting into that Resilient Zone as often as we could. That means there is always a bit of residual stress left in the system.

When Our Systems Up-Regulate

When the events are intense or traumatic, our systems react as if we're under fire and we move to ward off the threat. We can activate up so that we find ourselves in a state of hyper-arousal or we may find ourselves numbed out into a state of hypo-arousal. Either direction takes us out of the Resilient Zone and places us at risk for physical and emotional distress. We can also enter into an alternating state of hyper- and hypo-arousal which may or may not be congruent with the actual events. For example, we may feel agitated when the agenda at a meeting is something ordinary like scheduling and find ourselves unable to feel anything when funding for our project is being debated.

The various states of arousal are shown in the figure below, adapted from the Trauma Resource Institute.

What happens under fire?

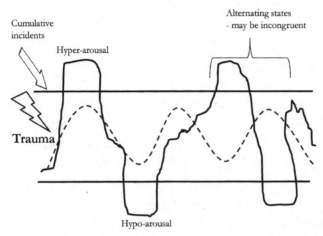

Diagram adapted from Trauma Resource Model courtesy Laurie Leitch & Elaine Miller-Karas

When our threat response system is activated we have three modes of reacting: fight, flight, and freeze. These responses are intended to deal with the threat and lower the potential for damage to ourselves. They are highly practiced, automatic stances we take which depend to varying degrees on our biological, psychological, and habitual patterns. The most important thing to remember is that at this stage of fight, flight, freeze, the response evoked is primarily from our biological nature. That is, it's the survival and reactionary portions of our brain taking over and running the show.

Fight. We enter into fight mode and respond with anger, aggression, or by pushing back against the perceived threat. When the threat is obviously against our physical safety, acting with aggression may be required. However, our social lives are more ambiguous. A driver who cuts us off on the highway, a colleague who isn't playing along as a team member, a boss who is not hearing our requests or our needs can each trigger reactions of anger. Our response reflects a need to establish space and position to feel safe.

Joe is a manager of a team of individuals who have to work under extreme pressure to produce high quality products in a very competitive market. He spends long hours at work and has little time for the things he enjoys. When he wakes up in the morning, in his mind, he's already at his desk trying to put out fires that either didn't get quenched the day before or have erupted overnight. He suffers with hypertension, is overweight, and has taken on a pre-emptive stance of anger and aggressive speech with his colleagues, boss, and even his family. Joe is a pragmatic and straight-talking person who had trouble believing that "just breathing" was going to do anything for his work or health situation.

Flight. When the flight mode is activated we look for ways to get out of the situation we find threatening. As we noted before, when the threat is obvious, like a truck coming at us, getting out of the way (fleeing) is a good thing. In social situations, however, threat may be perceived in the tone of voice, a decision about our position or power in a project, or something we believe we have no control over. We feel our only option is to get as far away from the threat as possible.

Evan is the executive assistant to a driven boss who takes no time explaining her expectations of the projects he is given to manage for her. He finds himself more and more helpless trying to figure out what is important and what is not. Events at work tend to create conflicting demands and Evan often finds himself in double binds. Eventually, things erupt into angry tirades from his boss and he finds himself feeling helpless to control things. He describes a cycle of trying to find ways to avoid going into work and, when he does go, coming home and drinking too much so he can numb the day's intense emotions.

Freeze. When the freeze mode is activated, our adaptive systems stop functioning. In some cases, we freeze or stop in order to slow down the per-ceived threat or hope that we will become invisible to the threat. Situations that trigger a freeze response are interesting (intellectually, that is) because they are marked by an absence of information. We freeze because we don't know what to do next.

Laura is a mental health professional who has been feeling over-whelmed by the complex cases she is treating. The institution she works in does not allow for any time to do complete assessments and the work-load measures are expected to reflect people moving through the system quickly. In her case, time and body counts are money for the administra-tors. In each interview, Laura feels stuck when she tries to conceptualize the case or formulate a treatment plan. She feels overwhelmed by what she doesn't know about each patient and the responsibility of making decisions with so little information.

Each of these reactions evoked by Joe, Evan, and Laura's situations reflects a reality that they are trying to manage. We need to see the power of the physiological system when the feelings are triggered and not take that on as an enduring character flaw in ourselves.

Up to this point, we are responding from a deep animal sense of needing to preserve our well-being. In the next section, we will see how the thinking patterns kick in and ramp the physiology up. We also see how mindfulness practice can interrupt this process and ground us so that we can take more skillful action.

The Appraisal System

Although a part of the reactions faced by Joe, Evan, and Laura are based in biology, they also reflect each of their assumptions about what might happen to them if they don't respond efficiently or well. There is no question that a threat can be real; losing one's job, family ruptures, and personal distress sadly are all facts of our life. Researcher Bruce McEwen (author of *The End of Stress as We Know It*) describes this cumulative stress which leads to a breaking point as an *allostatic load* – a point where the system stops adapting to the strains that "load" onto it. However, in the moment of the assault, we have more options than we may believe we do. Our appraisal or interpretation of the event, what it means to us, plays a very significant role in how we respond to it.

We tend to respond to situations not just for what they are (the truck coming at us, the boss yelling, the children fighting in the back of the car). We also layer on the experience a meaning *about* the event. The demanding job is tough enough to deal with but Joe is also very aware that, in this economy, he can't afford to lose his job. When the situation escalates (along with his blood pressure), his thoughts also ramp up into catastrophes about being homeless and unable to care for his family. Evan's thinking patterns run along lines of being weak and unable to stand up for himself. He sees his career plummeting and his future seems hopeless. Laura begins to have obsessive thoughts about being sued by her patients or losing her job because she will be assessed as incompetent.

The situations are bad enough and tough to deal with just as they are.

However, the negative thinking spirals each of them out so that there is no chance of being steady in the face of the problem. Another way of saying this is that the frontal lobes go off-line, our problem-solving tanks, and our options narrow down to the physiological autopilot. Popping out of the Resilient Zone, the inevitable happens: Joe explodes, Evan avoids, and Laura gets stuck.

Thoughts Make the Thinker

If your house is flooded or burnt to the ground, whatever the threat to it, let it concern only the house. If there's a flood, don't let it flood your mind. If there's a fire, don't let it burn your heart. Let it be merely the house, that which is outside of you, that is flooded or burned. Now is the time to allow the mind to let go of attachments.

Our Real Home - A talk by Ajahn Chah

We become attached to having things go a certain way. When they don't, we tend to push back, cling, or get confused. Caught in this trap, we see blame and shame as reflecting who we are and not what is unfolding. We take ownership of the other person's assumptions and add them to our own self-criticism and negativity about ourselves. Becoming skillful in difficult situations requires practice in changing the negative thinking patterns that can quickly spiral us out into dark moods of hopelessness and helplessness. To use our metaphor of trains, thought patterns are the trains we get on. Our job is to notice we have and get off as quickly as we can. Only then will the many skillful ways to deal with distress open up for us.

An Appropriate Response

Before we talk more about skillful ways to meet our challenging situations, let's clarify what it means to be skillful in the face of a threat. There's a misconception that mindfulness means we have to respond in some kind of sweet and kind way when we're confronted with anger, demands, or ignorance. Not so! That just makes us vulnerable to further assaults. A mindful response is an appropriate response to the situation. If we think of anger, running away, and being stuck or indecisive as the first stage of meeting a difficult situation, skillful actions form a continuum from that set of responses.

Practicing mindfulness of our body, emotions, and sensations means we have a level of awareness that permits more and more skillful choices. We move away from the knee-jerk anger towards appropriate forcefulness and even further towards asserting our needs or point of view. Instead of fleeing the situation, we can see a path to distancing from the intensity of the moment, walking away from the situation and eventually suggesting that a "time out" to consider the situation may be useful. When faced with insufficient information to make a decision, we may begin by withdrawing ourselves from the threat and learn how to wait for the necessary information to emerge.

Our thoughts create an internal environment from which our actions can arise. If that internal environment is one of uncertainty about our competence, fears about our future, or shame about our past, we should not then be surprised that our actions will be unpredictable, restricted, or tentative. The judgmental mind is powerful in shaping our needs and actions to protect ourselves from blame and shame. Recognizing this cycle of inner and outer connection is the first step of mindfulness. Pausing and taking note of the thoughts that arise is the second step. Then with practice, we can begin to peel ourselves away, unhook ourselves, from the thoughts and feel some relief from them. Mindfulness teachers like to say, "Thoughts are not facts." We prefer to work with the idea that even if a thought is a fact, it may be our reaction to it that is getting us into trouble.

Responsive Not Reactive

For example, it may be true that Joe, Evan, Laura might lose their jobs and that would place them and their families at some risk. However, it does not mean they are worthless, weak, or incompetent. Nor does it mean that they definitely will lose their jobs if they set limits. A mindful approach makes it possible to get past the judgmental nature of our thinking. As Joe, Evan, and Laura developed their awareness of their thinking patterns, they began to see different ways to take stands or organize their work so that it was manageable and even fulfilling. Ultimately they were able to see that if it happened, the job loss was only a job loss, not a loss of character.

The next figure shows how the system responds as we become more skillful in our practice.

Mindfulness & Respons-ability

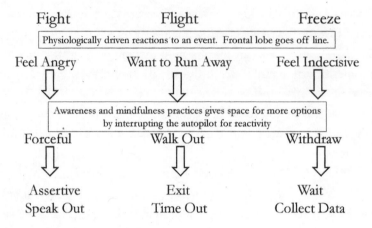

Fight	Flight	Freeze
Physiologically driven reactions to an event. Frontal lobe goes off line.		
Feel Angry	Want to Run Away	Feel Indecisive

Awareness and mindfulness practices gives space for more options by interrupting the autopilot for reactivity

Forceful	Walk Out	Withdraw
Assertive	Exit	Wait
Speak Out	Time Out	Collect Data

Cultivating Compassionate Awareness of Our Thoughts through the Five Skillful Habits

Cultivating awareness of our thought patterns using the Five Skillful Habits is very similar to our previous practices. However, we may feel a bit more challenged on this platform of mindfulness because it's hard not to believe every thought that flies by. We use our mind and its contents to solve complex problems so it's hard to consider that such a power house of information processing can be the source of our problems as well.

Respecting our mortality by attending to our thinking can mean bringing awareness to the way our bodies respond to what we say to ourselves internally. Self-talk can be nourishing when done with respect, but can be debilitating when it is denigrating or self-defeating. Yet, we feel free to say things to ourselves that diminish our worth and question our value.

Generosity towards our inner experiences is similar to our emotional and sensational experiences. Allowing the thought to be there without arguing with ourselves is a useful stance. It prevents endless debates with ourselves that we are bound to lose. Acknowledging that we have a tendency to be hard on ourselves opens the door to being compassionate with ourselves.

Setting limits on the path we take through our thoughts is one of the most important skills to cultivate. We know the consequences of constant negativity. Not only does it become a well-worn path, it also becomes the fall-back position when we are scared or tired. The spiral down into depression or out into anxiety is easy to form and gentle awareness of the early stages of the spiral allows us to disengage before it becomes too steep.

Compassionate speech is also an important skill to cultivate with regard to our thought patterns. The only way to break a harmful pattern is to stop the old pattern **and** to foster a new one. When we notice the negative thought, we are on our way to opening a space where are can be more supportive of who we are. It's worth repeating that the point is not to engage in meaningless self-affirmations. The practice is to widen our scope of experience and notice that there are many thoughts that come and go: pleasant, unpleasant, and neutral. From this vast array, we can choose what is necessary in the moment to encourage and sustain our practice of well-being.

Mindful consumption in the realm of thoughts will be noticing that wide banquet of stimuli which activate our thinking. Not only is it important to re-configure our thinking with respect to ourselves so that we are not self-consuming negativity, we need to pay close attention to the external stimuli which can activate negative spirals. Media images, stories, assumptions about our skills and capacity all have an impact on what we think about ourselves and others. It is important therefore to discern among all the offerings, inner and outer, so that we are not on a slippery slope into ill-health.

As before, in the table attached, we have listed examples of behaviours that cultivate each skillful habit. Remember that we are in a paradox of using our thinking function to shape our thinking patterns. When you decide on a skillful habit you would like to focus on for this week and which activity suits you, be aware that this is a great opportunity to train our discernment of well-being.

Continuing Your Practice

BEST Meditation Practice the meditation every day this week. Integrate the platforms of Body, Emotions, Sensations, and Thoughts. Use the Record of Daily Practice in Chapter 3.

Breathing Space Meditation Practice as often as you can this week. Use the breath as a means of approaching tension and a way of un-hooking from the runaway thoughts.

Mindful Bells Continue to practice with various stimuli in your environment to bring you back to the breath.

Five Skillful Habits Select a habit to cultivate this week. Choose a habit that you feel encourages you to be compassionate with yourself. In the template, create a list of sensation words that you are particularly familiar with. Practice observing how they change.

Five Skillful Habits to Cultivate for Thoughts

Habit to train	Training examples
1. Respect for mortality	Note negative thoughts
2. Generosity	Allow thoughts to come and go (allow yourself to hop off trains)
3. Respect of limits	Notice when your thoughts are dictating your limits rather than your body (e.g. I can't do this)
4. Compassionate speech	Accept the thoughts as they are, just thoughts
5. Mindful Consumption	Note thoughts while eating (e.g. I shouldn't, I'm fat, what will my next bite taste like)

CHAPTER 7:
Sustaining Well-Being Through Compassion

Our intention in this chapter: We visit the intention of practice. What brought us to the point of suffering is the belief that we are separate, separate from who we are and separate from all others around us. As we become aware of the fragility of our inner and outer environment, we feel motivated to be steady in the face of its impermanence. We also see the interconnectedness of our lives with each other and how our concepts and ideas get in the way of living skillfully. As we peel away the suffering arising that this belief of separateness causes, we are left with the realization that only kindness can be the outcome of practice.

Falling Forward, Falling Back

The last six weeks of practice have been focused on cultivating a steadiness in the face of the constant change in our lives. Whether it is obvious or not, our lives are eternally evolving and moving in many directions all at once. With the momentum of our assumptions and beliefs, we tend to fall forward into that life, not always noticing whether those assumptions and beliefs are serving us well. In counterpoint, when our lives take a trajectory that generates pain and suffering, we fall back into old habits of rejecting the negative, clinging to the positive, and feeling confused about what is uncertain.

Mindfulness practices help us restore our balance so that the processes of falling forward and falling back become turning points and not endpoints. This is an important point in mindfulness practice: we can't avoid the dance, but we can learn to be in rhythm with the music. To do that, it's important to practice so that we can prevent relapse into old habits and sustain our well-being.

Let's first say a few words about relapse prevention. The conventional definition of relapse is the recurrence of symptoms following a reduction to sub-clinical levels of the disorder. For example, depression relapse means symptoms of depression go away and then recur. When we apply mindfulness practices to managing our emotional states, we can include cultivating a gentle awareness of the signals of our experiences with psychological distress. As we mentioned in the chapter on sensations, we attend to the sensations in our body and suspend our tendency to label them as symptoms. By working with the sensations at this early stage, we may avoid a panicked spiral that escalates the sensations into full-blown symptoms.

Susan, for example, attended to her sensations of fatigue and lower moods; she worked at staying with the sensations with a gentle and open stance. This was hard for her because her experience of depression and pain was so powerful that she wanted to do anything to avoid a relapse. Slowly, she learned that the critical relapse to prevent is falling back into the assumptions that a down day means an impending depression or feeling tired means a recurrence of debilitating fatigue.

Other participants also learned that kind welcoming of the feelings and sensations lead to an opening of their hearts to whom they are in this moment. We believe that this is the crucial point in practice. We begin to see who we are beyond the categories and labels of illness and character flaws. At one level we are coming back to Rumi's teachings of "welcome them all" – the dark thought, the shame, the meanness. At another level, we are practicing a non-discriminatory connection with whatever shows up in our awareness.

The Dance of Practice

Sustaining well-being is very important to the practice of relapse prevention of clinical disorders. It seems an obvious idea but too often we hope that having done a course or having learned intellectually about our ill-being will be enough to change its course. We call that riding the wave of good karma; positive intentions to understand our suffering can carry us along for a while. Because waves tend to flatten out, it doesn't last unless we put in the time to cultivate well-being too. In other words, it is crucial that we consider every moment as an opportunity to prevent relapse into past ineffective actions, speech, and ways of being. So let's look at three ways we can do that.

Embodying Practice

The first approach to sustaining well-being is to understand that practice becomes embodied as we do it. The path is created by walking it. When we first come into this form of practice, we are caught up in the concrete aspects of it. Learning how to sit, pay attention, do things in ways that are different from our usual activities probably took up most of our energies. At this stage we speak of having a practice. It's easily described, has a form, and we feel we can wrap our minds around it. It's a great place to start and it's important to see that, at this stage, it is something outside ourselves. There is a "me" and that "me" has a "practice."

As we progress, what we do goes deeper into our way of being. It becomes a process, a verb. We talk about *"going to practice"* mindfulness, we feel it is part of our transition from moment to moment. Among all the things we do, practicing mindfulness takes its place as something we engage in to enhance our well-being. It's now becoming part of the flow of our lives, the beginning of a way of being.

As we continue to deepen our commitment to well-being, the concepts of "me" with a "practice" and "me" going "to practice" fall away. *Practicing* becomes a seamless way of meeting our experience. We learn the many rhythms of our life and adapt to whatever music is playing. We see the edges of our life as the place where creativity and growth occur. The pain is there and it becomes a nudge towards well-being rather than an obstacle. We transform our unskillful ways of meeting our experience into an open-hearted stance to it.

This progression is not something we can force or plan out. It emerges out of a consistent and continuous practice. And, it requires setting our intention and effort in the direction of well-being.

Using the North Star

The second approach to sustaining well-being is the element of appropriate effort and direction in practicing. Zen Master Thich Nhat Hanh describes the Five Mindfulness Trainings of Buddhist practice (in our case, the Five Skillful Habits) as being a North Star that guides our practice. The point of using the North Star is to keep us on course; it is not about getting to the North Star. In other words, we aspire to live out our intentions and not live up to some ideal of practice or of life. Even in living out our intentions, it's important to remember that we are constantly adjusting our course and adapting to circumstances. Again, practice is in the letting go of concepts like "good" or "perfect." For example, if our intention is to get to the grocery store, we pay attention to the route we take and stay alert for detours or minor adjustments in our path there.

There are three commitments we make in order to sustain well-being. The first is *practicing continuously* . Potential participants who come to the information sessions ask how many hours they should put aside to do the homework. We tend to be very straightforward in answering this question: 24/7. Practice is a constant returning to what is happening in this moment. In that sense, it is continuous and seamless.

The second commitment is to see *practice as complete*. Zen artist and scholar, Kazuaki Tanahashi, teaches that an enso (a Zen circle drawn in one stroke of the brush) contains the perfect and imperfect. In that sense, it is complete. So it is with practice. It will contain the perfect and the imperfect. It will have moments of sloppiness and of single-pointed concentration. It will always be complete.

The third commitment is to *look up* to the horizon. In a moment of pain, we tend to fold over and become clutched around our pain. This is the source of our suffering. When we lift our vision up from what has captured us, we see the larger context of what we are experiencing. There may be pain and there is also a multitude of other experiences that are occurring at the same time. Buddhist teacher Tara Brach speaks of being caught in the trance of our experience. Looking up from that experience breaks the trance and opens up the possibility of meeting it differently.

The Four Aspects of True Love

The third approach to sustaining well-being is the practice of Love – for ourselves and others. Love is an interesting word. It tends to conjure up feelings of warmth and comfort in some instances. At other times, it may generate feelings like something sticky and cloying. Our life experience may have opened us to a freedom and safeness[5] in giving and receiving love. Or, it may have closed us down, tending not to trust the word or actions that supposedly represent being loved. It's important that we respect our approach-avoidance of the word, what it triggers, and its deep meaning for us. The term "Love" is also used in a proprietary way in Western culture. We reserve it for close family and friends, often feeling suspicious if it's used in casual situations. As you can see, it's a loaded word weighted down with assumptions about relationships.

There is another perspective of love which has nothing to do with arousal, attachment, or obligation. It is a practice of being present to ourselves and others in a way that is nourishing and supportive. When we practiced the Five Skillful Habits, we were cultivating an ethical approach to our body, speech and mind. In a very solid way, we are cultivating the mind of non-preferential love for ourselves and others. This way of practicing allows us to become more open, create safeness, and feel resilient as we engage in our lives.

The practice of love is made up of four stances: lovingkindness, resonant joy, compassion, and equanimity. Let's look at each.

---

5   *Safeness* is a term used by Paul Gilbert who developed Compassion-Focused Therapy. It refers to creating an inner state of comfort and self-soothing which is solid because it does not depend on external factors.

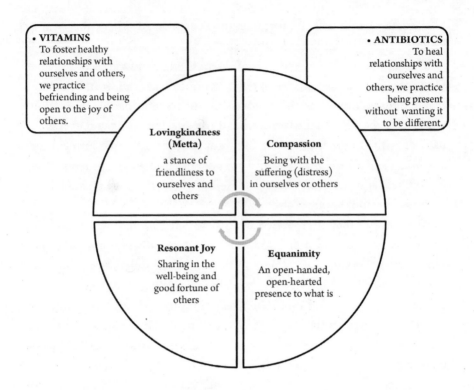

- **VITAMINS**
  To foster healthy relationships with ourselves and others, we practice befriending and being open to the joy of others.

- **ANTIBIOTICS**
  To heal relationships with ourselves and others, we practice being present without wanting it to be different.

Lovingkindness (Metta)

a stance of friendliness to ourselves and others

Compassion

Being with the suffering (distress) in ourselves or others

Resonant Joy

Sharing in the well-being and good fortune of others

Equanimity

An open-handed, open-hearted presence to what is

Lovingkindness (metta) is a willingness to befriend ourselves and others unconditionally and non-preferentially. When we practice a lovingkindness, or metta, meditation (as we will this week), we begin with a wish for ourselves to feel safeness, health, and well-being. It's not magic. It is an opportunity to open to the possibility that we might be able to feel safeness, health, and well-being. This can be a difficult concept because, for the most part, we tend to live in fear of old age, sickness, and death. We believe that we need to keep the door to our heart and mind firmly shut against these things that lead to a deterioration of well-being. When we practice metta, we are opening the door we keep shut against being hurt by the impermanence of all things. Initially, that door may only open a crack. But as the Leonard Cohen song goes, that's how the light gets in.

Slowly, in our meditation, we widen the circle of lovingkindness to those who are close to us, who are in need of care, who are part of our landscape, who may have hurt us, all who share with us the vulnerability to aging, illness, and death.

Resonant Joy is the capacity to take delight in the joy of others. It is usually called sympathetic joy; we prefer the concept of resonating with another's happiness just as a tuning fork vibrates to the same pitch as the instrument it is tuning. Joy is infectious, unavoidable when we are in its authentic presence. Sometimes it may be difficult to feel joy in another's accomplishments because we are so deeply trained to be competitive or to look at everything through the mind of poverty. We believe there is only a limited amount of things to have. Because our understanding of progress in life is categorical and linear, when someone else gets something or progresses to the next milestone, we feel robbed or blocked.

The practice of cultivating resonance with another's joy slices through the preferential mind. Within limits, the source or object of the person's joy is not the focus of the resonance. That just breeds envy. Our joy is generated simply by seeing the immense capacity we all have to experience boundless joy.

Lovingkindness and ***Resonant Joy*** are the vitamins we take to keep ourselves healthy, day by day, moment by moment. They replenish us and create a steadiness with which we can meet the difficult and the unwanted.

Compassion is the capacity to be present to the suffering of ourselves and others. It begins with a willingness to witness the pain within and in front of us. Bearing witness to suffering is a powerful practice and requires us to let go of needing to fix things. We usually race into fix-it mode because we have a hard time sitting with our own suffering. It's important to remember that resonance with another's joy means we also resonate with their suffering. So, compassion and resonant joy are partners in cultivating a loving relationship with ourselves and others.

The practice of compassion requires a steadiness within ourselves so that we do not look away from the suffering in front of us. Over the last few years, people everywhere have lived through and continue to live with many heart-rending situations. Earthquakes, tsunami, hurricanes, politically-motivated attacks, and the ever-present issues of poverty and disease leave us feeling helpless when we are inundated with stories, images and sounds of tragedy. Thankfully, compassion flows in from all parts of the world for the people and all beings who are experiencing such intense suffering. Yet, that pull towards the pain of the world has to be balanced with self-compassion or burn out is inevitable.

Self-compassion has been explored wonderfully by Drs. Paul Gilbert, Christopher Germer, and Kristen Neff. Their books are listed in our Reference section. Collectively, they view self-compassion as a kind and open-hearted stance we take to our body, thoughts, and emotions. They each discuss the need to become aware of our harsh inner critic that triggers the shame and blame stance we have toward our experiences.

Take a moment and look back over the practices of the last few weeks. You may notice that they have been ways of attending to our experience without engaging in the story-telling. These are the beginnings of self-compassion: noticing a negative thought and not absorbing it as an absolute truth, feeling a sensation of pain and allowing it be just that, holding a welling of emotion and breathing steadily with it. These are moments that we had in which we took the opportunity to treat ourselves more humanely, with more kindness, and were willing to sit compassionately with who we are.

Often, participants in the course will ask whether this form of being self-compassionate is really egoism or self-indulgence. That's a terrific question because it cuts to the essence of mindful practice. How do we find the balance between self-compassion and its near enemies, self-promotion and self-indulgence? How can we know whether we are being appropriately caring of others or posturing our mindful muscles? What's the difference between appropriately caring for ourselves and taking the easy way out? These are challenging questions and the answer lies in how honest we are about our intentions. As you may see, it is a quick slide from self-compassion to holding our mindful practice up as a barrier against authentic relationships. We can claim we are above the ordinary problems of the world because our day is packed with "mindful moments"; we call this mindful bypassing of our experience. Our language gets peppered with jargon like "I'm just being"; we talk the talk but likely trip when we walk. Or we race off from retreat to retreat to keep the high of blissing out; it can be competitiveness with others in what we think is a race to enlightenment.

These tactics become ways of fostering an entitlement to continue living the way we always have or they can be ways of competing with others whom we judge as doing more or less than we do as "mindful" practitioners. When this happens, we lose sight of the intention of practice which is to bring us closer to our deep interconnections with each other and ourselves.

Equanimity is the even-handed stance to whatever is unfolding in the moment. It is the antidote to the preferential mind which wants what isn't and rejects what is. When we meet our experience without a pre-meditated idea of how it should go or what it will bring us, we are liberating ourselves from all limitations. These limitations are set by the experiences in our past and our hopes for a different future. Equanimity allows us to stay with our experience just as it is and to see it clearly, unfiltered by desires, craving or anxiety.

It is important to note that equanimity is not a passive acceptance or a blasé stance to what we are going through. That would just be another mindful bypass of our real experience. True equanimity is being fully aware that arising feelings are unpleasant and we are not willing to be distracted from them or seek to move away before we fully grasp the nature of our experience. In other words, we are not engaging in suppression or denial.

Compassion and *Equanimity* are the healing medication for us when we are suffering; sometimes we call them the antibiotics for the imbalance between ill- and well-being. When we are suffering, it is important to be able to bear witness to it without rushing in to fix it. This holds true for the suffering of others as well. And it is especially the case when we are ailing that we cultivate equanimity towards the illness. In relationships, equanimity is a key factor in support. When someone we love becomes ill, it is easy to say, "This isn't what I planned on as a relationship!" Equanimity allows us to pierce that preferential mind and be present for both our suffering.

Together the Four Aspects of Love make up a healing pill – if a somewhat large one to swallow! It is easy to see that relationships cannot function without building the foundations of kindness and joy which give us energy and willingness to pour on the compassion and equanimity when required.

Shadow Knowledge

It's also important to point out the "shadow" side of these stances to relationship. The danger of slipping into self-promotion in the practice of lovingkindness, resonant joy, compassion, and equanimity underlies the reason we have the Five Skillful Habits as a guideline for our behavioural practices. When we cultivate actions that are aware of our mortality, generous, careful of our limits, speech and consumption, we are making a commitment to live a balanced life. It doesn't mean a saintly or holier-than-thou life; it means we are aware of the suffering that is caused by not being aware of the consequences of our choices. The Five Skillful Habits become a way of guiding us so that we are self-caring in our choices and therefore have the energy to also be caring of others.

Cultivating Compassionate Well-Being through the Five Skillful Habits

Cultivating well-being through the Four Aspects of Love using the Five Skillful Habits begins with ourselves. As you may notice in the meditation, we begin with a wish for well-being for ourselves first. Then as we are steady in giving ourselves a sense of safeness that is independent of the push and pull of events, we stretch that compassion muscle to include those close to us and so on.

Respecting our mortality , we attend to our life as it is, with equanimity and compassion when we may be fearful about its limits and with resonant joy and lovingkindness when we can see each moment as a gift.

Generosity is a practice that opens us to all the ways in which we can take care of ourselves and others. It doesn't mean huge gestures; sometimes a simple act of kindness is sufficient. In fact, when we can titrate our giving to just what is needed, we conserve our energies and allow the well of generosity to refill steadily.

Setting limits is the flip side of being generous. It is often said that "No" is the most generous thing we can offer. As contrary as it may seem, when we offer to do what we can, we are likely more effective and we also allow others to have a chance to pitch in.

Compassionate speech is also an important skill to cultivate with regard to neutralizing our harsh inner critic and judgmental mind. It is also a way of soothing the preferential mind; when we want what we don't have or don't want what we have, we turn to ways to reassure ourselves that we have the capacity to meet these moments with equanimity.

Mindful consumption is another form of being compassionate with our ability to absorb all forms nourishment. It can range from eating foods that sustain well-being in our inner and outer systems to connecting with relationships or events with awareness of their impact on our ability to continue to live compassionately.

Continuing Your Practice

Metta Meditation Practice the lovingkindness meditation every day this week.

Breathing Space Meditation Practice as often as you can this week. Use the breath as a means of interrupting the shame/blame process and bringing awareness to your need for lovingkindness, compassion, equanimity or joy.

Mindful Bells Continue to practice with various stimuli in your environment to bring you back to the breath.

Five Skillful Habits Select a habit to cultivate this week. Choose a habit that you feel encourages you to be compassionate with yourself and others.

CHAPTER 8:
Preparing For The Next Chapter

Our intention in this chapter: We prepare for the next chapter of our lives.

Nothing Changes

In our waiting room, we have a little sign that says

Nothing changes if nothing changes

Sometimes we think our clients don't really need to meet with us. Just reading the sign seems to have a huge impact on many of them. At one level, we all understand the reality that everything changes. Our difficulties arise when we assert our preferences of what should and should not change. We also would prefer that things change in ways that suit what we want from life. Through our practice of mindfulness, we have challenged these views and perhaps learned to take a more compassionate stance to our distress when things change unpredictably and sometimes not in our favour.

When our clients share what struck them about the sign, they talk about their fear of change. After all, it was change that brought us to this place of suffering. It was change that took away the things we held dear: relationships, jobs, capacity to live fully, well-being. We believe these things define us, give us identity, motivation, satisfaction, and a sense of accomplishment. When their presence in our lives is threatened, we feel something fundamental is threatened. We feel fear and, naturally, fight back.

The idea that change is the essence of living is hard to accept in the middle of turmoil and distress. The autopilot reaction is to hold fast to what seems to be changing in the hope that we can keep the inexorable from happening. It's this behaviour of holding fast that the second "nothing changes" in the sign points to. And when "nothing changes," when we hold tightly to what we want, we continue to suffer; that's the first "nothing changes." So we could re-write the sign to read: we perpetuate our suffering when we hang on to the things we think define us.

It's loses a bit in the analysis, doesn't it?

As we work with the practice of Wise Mindfulness, we learn that change **is** living. It is what creates life and it is the only way in which we can experience our life. We learn that what absolutely has to change is our commitment to cultivating a healthier perspective of our situation. We tap into a deeper sense that an inner shift has to occur if we are going to get through the challenge of illness, divorce, anxiety about our children or loss of a job. In the middle of all the change that has happened, it seems almost ironic that creating deeper change is what will lead us to well-being. That change is the relationship we have with our body and mind.

The Four Platforms of Our Experience

Our practice together began with bringing awareness to our body. We attended to the sensations and learned to be non-judgmental about them. As we sat with the ever-changing experience of the body, moment by moment, we learned to listen carefully, to suspend our stories about what it could mean to have this or that sensation arise. As challenging as it may have been, we brought ourselves back into contact with our physical nature. We dropped into the way our body contains the entirety of what we experience and informs us of that experience.

We progressed through the sometimes-turbulent waters of our emotional nature and learned how to be present to the full range of emotions we experience. This can be one of the toughest parts of our journey on the mindful path to well-being. We do love to hold onto to our emotions as a means of showing and justifying our actions and attitudes. To begin to see our emotions as labels of sensory states and as habitual ways of perceiving relationships can be liberating – and a little bit frightening.

As we dove deeper into our experience, we learned to take a different stance, to listen differently to our emotions. If the body speaks to us through sensory perceptions, and emotions are a summary statement of these sensory perceptions, then it makes sense (pardon the pun) to go to the source of our experience. We practiced gentle and open awareness of the sensations in the body as they arose and let them go as they dispersed. We also practiced accepting the perennial return of these sensations, opening the door each time they knocked and closing it behind them when they left.

And finally, we entered the wispy world of our concepts and assumptions about our life, our identity, our view of how the world works. We challenged ourselves to consider that nothing can be fully known and that our perceptions tend to push us into certain stances. More than that, our perceptions are fuelled by our feelings of vulnerability, by how threatened we feel, by our biologically-set and nurture-trained tendencies to react by fighting, fleeing or freezing. Mindfulness practices don't change the building blocks of our nature; however, they do give us that momentary pause to intercept the autopilot behaviours.

When we felt overwhelmed by our experience, we may have lost our grounding and got on those trains in the hope of outrunning the distress. Our practices of mindful breathing, non-judgmental awareness, and gentle reminding (mindful bells) got us off those trains and back to the platform. As we practice, we also realized that the four platforms are really only one – experiencing *what is* .

Five Skillful Habits

Our framework to practice was the Five Skillful Habits of respect for life/mortality, generosity, respect for physical and emotional limits, mindful or compassionate speech, and mindful consumption. As we have learned, practice is not mindful without understanding our choices as ethical ways of interacting with the world. Each of these commitments allowed us to observe and cultivate a gentle awareness of how to make healthy choices, moment by moment, breath by breath.

Practicing within a framework of ethics is not meant to be oppressive.

In fact, it releases us from the prison of our reactivity. We begin to notice the ways in which we are so harsh with ourselves, how we drive ourselves relentlessly, and how we create and feed the source of our suffering. Grounding ourselves in the basic principles of mindful living gives us the space and capacity to choose wisely especially when things feel pressured and on the edge of tipping over into chaos.

Self-Compassion

Cultivating compassion for ourselves and for others is the food of Wise Mindfulness. We tend to view kindness and love with suspicion. There's a tendency to prefer to use a stick rather than a carrot to encourage us along in our aspirations. Of course, some of us also tend to use our carrots as a stick. Just as no good deed goes unpunished in our inner court of law, every success becomes a new measure of a level below which we cannot fall. Practicing self-compassion is something new to most of us but it quickly becomes a favourite. And no wonder! It actually feels good and replenishes us so that we can afford to give to others freely and with abandon.

It's also important to respect our reluctance about being kind to ourselves. Kindness and compassion are not license to be lazy or get ourselves off the hook for irresponsible behaviours. This is where the Five Skillful Habits come into play. They are, in effect, compassionate ways to live.

The Ninth Class

The half-life of any mindfulness program is about 3 months. After the initial flush of peace and satisfaction, we tend to backslide into our old habits. It's human. This is where the role of a practice community is important and we encourage everyone to find a community, which can support his or her practice.

Usually, practice communities tend to be contemplative ones in a religious setting. Buddhist, Christian, Jewish, Muslim, and other faith communities are welcoming of new practitioners. There are also secular communities that practice together regularly. It's important to be open to the experience of these communities and to respect the ways in which each one practices. It is a very personal choice and the way in which we might resonate with a group is unpredictable. However, we encourage the exploration because practice is best cultivated in a group of like-minded people.

At the Ottawa Mindfulness Clinic, we offer the opportunity to practice as a group once a month and to join in the all-day sessions that occur with each cycle of classes. It's always wonderful to see past participants return and to share the evening or day with them. Look for similar gatherings of mindfulness program graduates locally or online.

If communities are not available, make a commitment to practice regularly. Set a time each day or at least once a week to sit for 20-30 minutes. Use online communities to encourage that commitment. Go to retreats; connect with teachers through their writings and audio or online talks. In other words, look for all the possibilities that will allow an ongoing practice.

This is the Ninth Class: The rest of our life.

May we live it in mindfulness and compassion for ourselves and all beings.

Appendix A

Pleasant and Unpleasant Experiences

PLEASANT EXPERIENCES

As best you can, bring your attention to events as they happen and notice those that may be mildly unpleasant. Notice the sensations of the experience and record your impressions.

Describe the event	What sensations did you notice in your body during the unpleasant experience?	Was there a place in your body where the sensations were most noticeable?	Describe any emotions or thoughts that you noticed.	What are you noticing now? Does anything change when you breathe into the sensation?
Day 1				
Day 2				
Day 3				

Day 4				
Day 5				
Day 6				
Day 7				

UNPLEASANT EXPERIENCES

As best you can, bring your attention to events as they happen and notice those that may be pleasant. Notice the sensations of the experience and record your impressions.

Describe the event	What sensations did you notice in your body during the pleasant experience?	Was there a place in your body where the sensations were most noticeable?	Describe any emotions or thoughts that you noticed.	What are you noticing now? Does anything change when you breathe into the sensation?
Day 1				
Day 2				
Day 3				

Lynette Monteiro, Frank Musten

Day 4				
Day 5				
Day 6				
Day 7				

Appendix B

Liberated Life Guide: How to Meditate

Our colleague, Maia Duerr, author and founder of the Liberated Life Project, has written a wonderful guide to meditation. Thanks to her generosity, we have a slightly edited version here for your use. Please visit Maia at http://liberatedlifeproject.com for insightful articles, fantastic tips on practice, and a weekly resource list.

First of all, let's start by talking about what meditation is and what it isn't.

There are a number of different kinds of meditation, including *zazen* (a Japanese word that means "sitting meditation"), *vipassana* (also known as insight meditation), and transcendental meditation (TM). Meditative practices are found in nearly all religious traditions, including Christianity and Judaism. All these forms of meditation are similar in many ways and different in a few ways.

The guidance I offer here is informed by my experience with Zen meditation over the past 15 years, but it's general enough that you should be able to work with it in your own life no matter what your spiritual orientation.

The most important thing to tell you about meditation, at least as I understand it, is that it's not a self-improvement program and not a relaxation program.

Meditation is about seeing reality more clearly and responding to your life from that place of clarity. You may find that some of the consequences are that you become more relaxed and better able to deal with stress, but the practice of meditation is *not* about tuning out. It's very much a tuning-in and waking up process.

As a result, you may find that things get worse before they get better.

You know that saying, "Ignorance is bliss"? Well, yes. But ignorance is the kind of bliss that can get you into trouble later on. A sincere and deep meditation practice can help you understand that awareness leads to the kind of bliss that sustains and nourishes us.

So if you're still game after knowing that, let's get to the heart of the matter – **how to practice meditation** .

1. *Create the conditions that will support your meditation practice.*

Perhaps most important of all, cultivate the mindset of making this a regular habit in your life. Meditation is most effective when you practice it on a consistent basis, ideally every day at the same time. It's better to make yourself sit down in your meditation space for a short period of time each day rather than skipping days and sitting longer amounts of time to make up for it. **Aim for consistency** .

There are three other conditions to pay attention to before you begin:

1.1 **Space:** Find a quiet space in your home and designate this as your meditation space. It helps if this is the only activity you do in this space. You may want to create a simple altar with objects that have special meaning for you – pictures of loved ones and people who inspire you, stones from a place in nature that nourishes you, and other sacred items.

In this space, set up your meditation cushion as well as a pad underneath it.

It's also fine to sit in a chair if you have physical limitations. But generally, it works best to sit on a cushion on the floor if you're able. I don't know any technical reason why this would be so, but my intuition tells me that being closer to the earth helps. Part of my own practice is about reminding myself that the earth supports me at all times, and by sitting on the ground I am literally feeling that truth in my body.

1.2 **Time:** It helps to meditate at the same time each day so that you can establish it as a habit. Some traditions consider the hour before sunrise to be the most auspicious time for meditation. That's a bit too early for me, but I definitely find that it works best to meditate first thing in the morning before I do anything else. The longer I put it off, the easier it becomes to make excuses that I don't have time.

Choose an amount of time for your meditation period. If you're just beginning, I'd suggest 10 minutes as the minimum amount of time to allow your mind and body to settle. You can gradually increase from there. I find that a 25-minute sitting period is optimal for me; other people like to sit in 35- or 45-minute periods. Over a process of experimentation you'll find what's right for you.

There are some fancy, expensive meditation timers, but all I use is a simple digital kitchen timer which works great. The advantage of setting a timer is that you release yourself from the need to check a clock every so often.

1.3 **Intention:** We need a compelling reason to do anything, otherwise it's easy to lose our way and our energy. In the case of your meditation, find what it is that motivates you to take up this practice. Perhaps it's for your own well-being, or for a more peaceful world. This can become a touchstone you can return to when you feel frustrated or challenged by your practice. I find it really helpful to light a candle and incense at the start of my meditation period. There's something about sitting with the glow from a candle that helps remind me of my own inner strength and spirit, and that's a quality I want to cultivate during a meditation period.

2. *Find the posture that works for you.*

If you don't have physical limitations, it's best to sit on a cushion on the floor rather than on a chair. If you're sitting on a cushion, you have a couple of choices. One is to sit in the *seiza* position, which means that you sit on your knees, either using a meditation bench or putting your cushion in a vertical position. Seiza looks like this:

The other choices are to sit in a **full lotus or half lotus position** :

Full Lotus

Half Lotus

If you're new to meditation, the lotus positions are more challenging to hold for a long period of time, depending on how flexible you are. You may want to start out sitting in a chair or in the seiza position and ease your way into these.

In the kind of meditation I do, zazen, it's important to hold your body as still as possible throughout the meditation period and not react if you have an unpleasant sensation like an itch or an ache. In other types of meditation, this is not as critical. Even so, **it's good to practice staying with a sensation for as long as possible before you change your body posture.**

This may seem difficult at first, but this sensation can become an object of your meditation, and you can investigate it more thoroughly… look into the length and quality of the ache, notice how it changes over the course of your observation of it.

There's a life lesson here – meditation can help us have more resilience in the face of difficult circumstances. This physical practice is a reflection of that.

3. *And begin. Start by paying attention to your body.*

People often have the impression that meditation is all about the mind, but actually it's a very physical experience.

Breath and body go together in this practice, though often in our daily life we might not experience them in an integrated way. Meditation is all about bringing dualities into oneness... so this is a chance to work with your breath and connect it back to your body.

Pay attention to your posture, especially your spine. Visualize a thread going up from the base of your vertebrae, where your buttocks make contact with the cushion or seat of your chair, all the way through your spine to the top of your head and beyond that to the sky. Breathe gently into this thread and allow that breath to help your backbone naturally come into alignment, without too much effort.

My first Buddhist teacher, Roshi Joan Halifax, has a wonderful way of describing the posture used in meditation and how it translates to our life. In her book *Being With Dying* she writes:

> "All too often our so-called strength comes from fear, not love; instead of having a strong back, many of us have a defended front shielding a weak spine. In other words, we walk around brittle and defensive, trying to conceal our lack of confidence. If we strengthen our backs, metaphorically speaking, and develop a spine that's flexible but sturdy, then we can risk having a front that's soft and open, representing choice-less compassion...
>
> "How can we give and accept care with strong-back, soft front compassion, moving past fear into a place of genuine tenderness? I believe it comes about when we can be truly transparent, seeing the world clearly — and letting the world see into us."

So our aspiration with our posture is to embody a strong back and a soft front... resilience and strength tempered with openness and vulnerability.

4. *Now the fun begins.*

Yes, at some point your mind will become an issue….. Don't worry about this too much. The most important thing you can do to sustain your practice is to realize that what your mind is doing is completely normal. Don't get discouraged. Stay with it.

5. *So what do I do with my crazy mind and intense emotions?*

If you're doing it "right," meditation will churn up a lot of sludge from your unconsciousness. That's really the whole point – to bring those less conscious aspects of ourselves into the light of awareness.

This "sludge" might come in the form of a torrent of thoughts, perhaps not so pleasant:

- "I know I shouldn't have said that to my girlfriend!"
- "That a**hole! I can't believe he's treating me this way!"
- "How will I ever find a job that makes me happy?"
- "I can't stand my landlord!"
- "Did I remember to turn the iron off before I left?"

…and so on and so forth.

Once you've created more space through meditation you may also start feeling things that you've long suppressed. Or if you're going through a particularly difficult situation right now, meditation may open a floodgate of emotions.

All of this is okay… the practice is to simply witness these thoughts and feelings without getting swept away by them.

Again – there's an important life lesson here. Our practice is teaching us how to be present to the conditions of our life without feeling overwhelmed by them. And we are learning how to find a place of equanimity within, even if the outer circumstances of our life are in turmoil.

As a thought arises in your mind, see if you can get into the habit of simply noting it without entertaining it. (That's a funny expression, isn't it? "Let me entertain that thought.")

One way to do this is the practice of labeling your thoughts . You might notice that you tend to dwell on things in your past that you wish you had done differently. When these kinds of thought arise for me, I gently say to myself, "Re-playing," because what I'm doing is re-playing a past scene in my life, *ad nauseum* , just like a bad movie. You may find that you're planning for a future encounter or event. When this happens to me, I say, "Rehearsing."

You can use the same technique with emotions. You might note that you're feeling sadness, or anger, or even joy. All of them will rise up and pass away. **In the moment that you have labeled the thought or feeling, you have just had an experience of awareness** . Buddhist teacher Sharon Salzberg calls this "the magic moment." In this way, distraction during our meditation is actually a gift, not a curse. We get to practice being present to ourselves, over and over and over.

You can also use your body and breath as an anchor. One mantra that I use quite often during my meditation period is: "Come back home to my body; come back home to my breath." I say this to myself to help me return attention to my body and breath.

You may also want to try this sequence that I've adapted from Bhante Gunaratana's book, *Mindfulness in Plain English* :

5.1 Find your breath, become aware of the physical, tactile sensation of the air as it passes in and out of the nostrils. Pay special attention to the point just inside the tip of your nose. Use this point to keep your attention fixed.

5.2 Make no attempt to control your breath; simply observe its movement in and out past this point. Don't increase the depth of your breath or its sound.

5.3 Observe the breath closely, and allow yourself to be fascinated by its intricate movements, and by its variations: long breath, short breath, ragged breath, smooth breath, and more.

Caveat : There may be times when sitting meditation is actually not the best practice for you. If you're going through an extremely painful situation, like the recent loss of a loved one, the feelings that arise during meditation may be almost unbearable. I would advise giving yourself a break and not expecting yourself to endure that painful level of intensity in sitting meditation. I remember going through a difficult relationship break-up and feeling like I was about to explode with grief while I was sitting. A teacher advised me to do gentle walking meditation outside as a way to work with those powerful emotions in my body. That guidance was incredibly helpful… I realized I needed some kind of more active movement practice to process the intense feelings of anger and sadness I was experiencing. In a few weeks, I was able to resume sitting meditation.

6. *The payoff.*

Okay, I know that meditation isn't about having a goal to achieve. And yet I want to let you know that there are some really important reasons to start meditating and to sustain it over time.

I wrote about this in detail on this post but I'll cut to the chase here: the very best part of a meditation practice is that it helps us to see old patterns in our life much more clearly. **Because of this awareness, we have the ability to liberate ourselves from choices that make us suffer. And because of awareness, we increase our capacity to feel compassion, joy, and equanimity.**

Your life will change because of this practice. I guarantee it. And the longer you continue your practice over weeks, months, and years, the bigger the change will be. So keep on!

7. *Find a community of people with whom to sit.*

Practicing alone is good, but practicing with a group is even better. Because the heart of meditation practice is about realizing our interconnection with all beings and then understanding how to actualize this realization in our everyday lives, it *really* helps to sit with other people.

Also, when you connect with a meditation group, you may be able to find a spiritual teacher or mentor who can guide your meditation practice more closely. I encourage you to do so. The deeper you go into meditation, the more it helps to have a personal relationship with someone who has been through the same territory.

I hope that you find these suggestions useful in beginning or deepening your own sitting meditation practice. If you have questions that aren't addressed here, please let me know in the comments how I can support you.

And most importantly, simply begin your meditation practice… **it's never too late!**

Appendix C

Reading & Meditation Resources

Mindfulness-Based Stress Reduction & Mindfulness-Based Cognitive Therapy

Full Catastrophe Living: Using the wisdom of your body and mind to face stress, pain, and Illness
Jon Kabat-Zinn (Delta)
Wherever You Go, There You Are
Jon Kabat-Zinn (Hyperion Press)
Heal Thyself: Lessons on mindfulness in medicine
Saki Santorelli (Bell Tower)
The Mindful Way through Depression
J. Mark Williams, John D. Teasdale and Zindel V. Segal (Guilford Press)

Mindfulness & Meditation

Mindfulness in Plain English
Bhante Henepola Gunaratana (Wisdom Publications)
Breath by Breath
Larry Rosenberg (Shambala Publications)
The Blooming of a Lotus
Thich Nhat Hanh (Parallax Press)
The Miracle of Mindfulness
Thich Nhat Hanh (Parallax Press)

Buddhist Roots of Mindfulness Practice

The 4 Foundations of Mindfulness in Plain English
Bhante Gunaratana (Wisdom Publications)
Breathe! You Are Alive

Thich Nhat Hanh (Parallax Press)
Our Appointment with Life
Thich Nhat Hanh (Parallax Press)
Transformation and Healing
Thich Nhat Hanh (Parallax Press)

Lovingkindness & Self-Compassion

Radical Acceptance: Embracing your life with the heart of a Buddha
Tara Brach (Bantam)
Living With Your Heart Wide Open: How Mindfulness and Compassion Can Free You from Unworthiness, Inadequacy, and Shame
Steve Flowers and Bob Stahl (New Harbinger Publications)
The Mindful Path to Self-Compassion
Christopher Germer (Guilford Press)
Self-Compassion: Stop beating yourself up and leave insecurity behind
Kristin Neff (William Morrow)
Lovingkindness: The revolutionary art of happiness
Sharon Salzberg (Shambhala Publications)

Peace & Happiness

The Happiness Hypothesis: Finding Modern Truth in Ancient Wisdom: Why the meaningful life is closer than you think
Jonathan Haidt (Basic Books)
Happiness: A Guide to developing life's most important skill
Matthieu Ricard and Daniel Goleman (Little, Brown & Company)
Real Happiness: The power of meditation
Sharon Slazberg (Workman Publication)
Mindfulness: An eight-week plan for finding peace in a frantic world
Mark Williams and Daniel Penman (Rodale Press)

Workbooks

The Mindfulness & Acceptance Workbook for Anxiety
John Forsyth & Georg H. Eifert (New Harbinger Publications)
A Mindfulness-Based Stress Reduction Workbook
Bob Stahl & Elisha Goldstein (New Harbinger Publications)
The Mindful Path Through Shyness

Steve Flowers (New Harbinger Publications)

Mindful Eating

Eating Mindfully
Susan Albers (New Harbinger Publications)
Mindful Eating: A guide to rediscovering a joyful and healthy relationship with food
Jan Chozen Bays (Shambhala Publications)

Meditation Resources

Please see our website Resources page to order meditation CDs used in the book, for full page versions of the Daily Practice and Five Skillful Habits forms and for a list of software meditation bells and timers.

http://www.ottawamindfulnessclinic.com/programs/resources.html

Appendix D

The Goblet 3-Minute Meditation

This breathing exercise can be helpful to ground ourselves so we feel steady in the face of difficult or intense emotions. Our tendency is to get caught in the stories about the emotional content and to try and get out of it as quickly as we can. This can lead to impulsive choices or reactivity that feeds into a rapid cycle of more unpleasant emotions. Because the breath conditions our body and emotions, we can use that breath to bring us to a solid sensory platform from which we can observe and choose our actions with mindfulness.

Initially, you may wish to practice this as a 3-minute sequence. As you feel more fluent with the meditation, you can use it as a 3-breath sequence to step back and ground yourself in the face of intense emotions. If it helps to visualize the sequences, you may wish to picture a goblet: the bowl, stem and base form the three parts of focus for the breath awareness.

First minute: open your awareness to your experience. Open to everything in your sense field – touch, sight, sound, smell, taste, thoughts. Imagine it's a bowl in which everything is held without attraction or aversion. Be gentle with yourself, respecting your limits for being present to what is in your sense field. You may wish to visualize it as the bowl of the goblet.

Second minute: bring your attention to your breathing at your nostrils or abdomen. Feel the sensation of the breath. It may be the flow at the nostrils or the rise and fall of the belly. Bring the focus to the breathing just as it is. You may wish to visualize this narrowing as the stem of the goblet.

Third minute: ground yourself in the body. Bring your attention to your body, standing or sitting. Feel the floor under your feet if standing or the solidity of your seat if sitting. Sense into the solidity of the floor or chair, feeling it supporting you. You may wish to visualize this is the wide base of the goblet.

Gently guide your awareness to your surroundings. Take a deep in breath and a long slow out breath.

If you wish you may want to write down what you noticed in this practice.

Appendix E

Day of Mindfulness

Set aside a day to do this. Arrange for at least a period from mid morning to mid-afternoon, some time period that spans over the time you would have lunch. You can prepare the room and your food the night before or choose that preparation as part of your day of mindfulness. You can use the schedule below or create one that suits your needs.

Remember, this is not a marathon. It is not about gritting your teeth to prove you can get through a day of silence. Think of it as a chance to be with your own best friend, to encounter yourself anew, to rest your mind and heart. To do that, we suggest putting away all reading and writing materials. Guard your senses; avoid reading labels, titles on your bookshelf, etc. You can set up a talk for the afternoon if you wish. There are many available online or you can purchase CDs by various teachers.

Get a good night's sleep and when you wake up go through your normal routine (try not to have any caffeine drinks). At your appointed time, begin sitting. Use a guided meditation from a CD or just sit. Try to use a timer for your sitting so you are not looking at the clock constantly. Put a clock in a discrete place should you want to follow a scheduled day.

10 AM to 11 AM – start with two sitting meditations for 20-minutes (or 30 mins) and alternate with a 10 min period of walking meditation (See Appendix C for link to resources).

11 AM – mindful movements or yoga

1130 AM – prepare your lunch, walk outdoors, do the Body Scan, or sit again

12 PM – lunch – eat mindfully, attending to every sense – touch, taste,

sight, smell, sound.

1245 – do the dishes!

1300 – outdoors walking meditation or another sitting for 20 minutes

1330 – Listen to a talk from an online selection or a CD you may have for this occasion.

1430 – clean up and continue to enter your life moment by moment!

Limited Photocopy License

The publishers grant individual purchasers nonassignable permission to reproduce the Records of Daily Practice and Five Skillful Habits for Body, Emotions, Sensations and Thinking for personal use only. This permission is limited to the individual purchaser of this book.

This permission does not extend to the Pleasant and Unpleasant Experiences forms in Appendix A. For reprint permission of forms in Appendix A, please contact Guilford Press.

About the Authors

LYNETTE MONTEIRO, PHD, a clinical psychologist and Zen practitioner, was born in Burma and immigrated to Montreal in 1965. She graduated with her doctorate in psychology from the University of Ottawa where she conducted the first significant study of medication treatment of preschool-aged children with ADHD. Her private practice is composed of individual psychotherapy and conducting recruitment and professional advancement assessments for police services and military units. In 2003, she co-founded the Ottawa Mindfulness Clinic and began co-teaching Mindfulness-Based Cognitive Therapy (MBCT) courses with Frank Musten. In addition to MBCT training, she received training in Mindfulness-Based Stress Reduction (MBSR) at the Center for Mindfulness in Medicine, Health Care, and Society (Worcester MA) as well as Mindful Self-Compassion with Drs. Kristin Neff and Christopher Germer. As training director for the Ottawa Mindfulness Clinic, she administers and teaches the Foundations of Mindfulness-Based Interventions program for graduate students in clinical psychology and health care professionals. Lynette has co-facilitated Sangha Arana, a Zen Buddhist community, since 2004 and completed training in Buddhist Chaplaincy at the Upaya Zen Institute, Santa Fe NM with Joan Halifax Roshi in 2012.

FRANK MUSTEN, PHD, began his career as a research psychologist in the Canadian Forces and later worked for the Royal Canadian Mounted Police. He established his private practice in 1979 in Toronto working with various corporations and municipal organizations and in Ottawa as a clinical psychologist. He has taught at the Canadian Police College, offered several workshops in effective management and stress reduction, and published articles in Canadian Business Magazine. Frank co-founded the Ottawa Mindfulness Clinic in 2003 with Lynette Monteiro and began teaching Mindfulness-Based Cognitive Therapy courses. After obtaining training in Mindfulness-Based stress Reduction at the Center for Mindfulness in Medicine, Health Care, and Society (Worcester MA), he continued with further training in the use of sensorimotor treatment for PTSD. He has developed the Mindfulness for Burnout Resilience program and a specialized mindfulness program for military members. He is a supervisor for the professional training program at the OMC and, in his private practice, treats couples with relationship difficulties, individuals with depression, work-related stress, and military service members with PTSD. He practices Secular Buddhism and co-leads Sangha Arana, a Zen Buddhist community.

Index

Printed in Canada